THE
DOMINICAN
REPUBLIC

WESTVIEW PROFILES • NATIONS OF CONTEMPORARY LATIN AMERICA
Ronald Schneider, Series Editor

†Available in hardcover and paperback

THE
DOMINICAN
REPUBLIC

A Caribbean Crucible

SECOND EDITION

Howard J. Wiarda
and Michael J. Kryzanek

Westview Press
BOULDER • SAN FRANCISCO • OXFORD

Westview Profiles/Nations of Contemporary Latin America

The authors thank Kahn Travel Communications for providing six of the photos for the second edition.

Jacket/paperback cover photos: *top left*—Cove in the Samaña Bay region (*courtesy of Judy Pinter*); *top right*—Young Dominican baseball players (*courtesy of the Dominican Republic Tourism Promotion Council*); *bottom*—Typical house in Puerto Plata (*courtesy of the Dominican Republic Tourism Promotion Council*)

Published in 1992 in the United States of America by Westview Press, Inc., 5500 Central Avenue, Boulder, Colorado 80301-2877, and in the United Kingdom by Westview Press, 36 Lonsdale Road, Summertown, Oxford OX2 7EW

Library of Congress Cataloging-in-Publication Data
Wiarda, Howard J., 1939–
  The Dominican Republic, a Caribbean crucible / Howard J. Wiarda
and Michael J. Kryzanek.
    p. cm. — (Westview profiles. Nations of contemporary Latin
America)
  Includes bibliographical references (p.   ) and index.
  ISBN 0-8133-8235-1 — ISBN 0-8133-8236-X (pbk.)
  1. Dominican Republic. I. Kryzanek, Michael J. II. Title.
III. Series.
 F1934.W49 1992
 972.93—dc20   92-14476
                                                                    CIP

Printed and bound in the United States of America

The paper used in this publication meets the requirements
of the American National Standard for Permanence of Paper
for Printed Library Materials Z39.48-1984.

10   9   8   7   6   5   4   3   2   1

For our parents,

John and the late Cornelia Wiarda
and
Mary and the late Edward Kryzanek,

in loving appreciation
for all the help along the way

Contents

Tables and Illustrations

Foreword

Although no single country is truly "typical" of the diverse region we are accustomed to calling Latin America, a few do come close to approximating the norm. In a very fundamental sense this is what makes the Dominican Republic fascinating for the comparativist. Subtract the major Latin American states—Brazil, Mexico, and Argentina—and this larger half of a Caribbean island becomes quite representative of the twenty-odd nations remaining. Certainly, most of their problems and contradictions can be found in the Dominican Republic, albeit perhaps differing in scale and intensity. For example, during the past generation the Dominican Republic has experienced both the highly institutionalized authoritarian rule of the Trujillo regime—the first in this hemisphere to really merit the label "totalitarian"—and significant experiments with broad, participatory political democracy. Developments in the past third of a century alone have included nearly every major variation between these poles: a populist *caudillo*, radical reformism, regimes based on elite manipulation, and even civil war and foreign intervention. No wonder, then, that Dominican reality has been portrayed in widely differing terms depending not only on the political flood tide of the moment, but also on the ideological commitment of the particular analysts.

It is within this context that a profile of "a Caribbean crucible" takes on special significance as one of the most important case studies in our series Nations of Contemporary Latin America. No single conventional approach is suitable or sufficient for the entire range of Latin American experience, and none is appropriate for this complex little country alone. The authors have accepted the challenge of understanding the Dominican Republic on its own terms, then explaining it to a foreign readership in a way that will be meaningful. The authors have also successfully portrayed both the individuality of this country and its comparable features; in so doing they have set a high standard for other analysts to follow. Indeed, the conceptualization framing this inquiry reflects Professor Wiarda's well-deserved reputation as a leading theorist of Latin American development, for he is a creative synthesizer as well as a persuasive exponent of a most sophisticated and sensitive type of cultural relativism. Dr. Kryzanek contributes a perceptive familiarity with the nuances of Dominican culture and society as well as with the present-day political scene and the peculiar nature of Latin American political leadership—critically important in a country that is still governed by an octogenarian with roots in the pre-1961 Trujillo era. For the salient certainty is that the Dominican Republic will have to find new political leadership in, if not by, the mid-1990s.

In this thorough revision of their 1982 book, the authors both amplify and deepen, rather than merely update, their analysis. For if on the political side this has been a decade of more and even more Joaquín Balaguer—now in his sixth term as president—significant changes have taken place in the socioeconomic and international spheres. The Dominican Republic has striven hard and with considerable effect to increase tourism, to develop export-processing zones, and to diversify the economy through extractive activities in order to lessen dependence on sugar. Like other Latin American countries it has vigorously privatized state enterprises and attracted foreign investment in a moderately successful effort to reverse the economic crisis of the late 1980s. Although continuing dramatic income inequality may be an improvement over the explosive tensions generated at the turn of the decade by negative economic growth, migration to Puerto Rico and the United States continues, a fact evident in the growing Dominican presence in New York City. Back in the home country, Haitians flow across the long land border in ever larger numbers, driven by the dreary economic situation and dismal political life of Hispaniola's eastern half.

All of these factors remind Dominicans that they are part of a larger Latin American dynamic that impels their country defensively to play a major role in Caribbean affairs and to seek to benefit from subregional and regional economic integration programs. Indeed, as the long era of Balaguer winds toward its end, in a Caribbean where Haiti defies democratization and Cuba has been under Castro's brand of Communist rule for a third of a century, it is more important than ever to understand the Dominican Republic's very substantial if yet imperfect democracy.

In sum, all the actors of Latin American political drama are present in the Dominican story, along with many of the elements of tragedy. Clearly, racial tensions, the role of multinational corporations, and friction with neighboring countries—all treated with balance and insight in this study—are among the factors that make the Dominican Republic a microcosm of the Caribbean and Central America, if not all of Latin America. Yet even beyond the normal patterns for this region, the Dominican Republic, in its long colonial experience and relatively short life as an independent nation, has been subject to a series of intense international pressures going back to sixteenth-, seventeenth-, and eighteenth-century conflicts among the imperial powers of Europe and their subsequent reflections during and after the Napoleonic Wars. In the present century the buffeted national life of the Dominican Republic reflects more clearly than that of any other country all of the key shifts in U.S. policy toward Latin America. Perhaps Wilson, Roosevelt, Kennedy, Johnson, and even Carter have left as lasting a mark on Dominican history as they have on their own country. This fact further accentuates the great importance of this particular volume to an appreciation of the actual Latin American situation.

Ronald M. Schneider
Queens College
City University of New York

Preface

The year 1492 was a momentous one in world history. In that year, Christopher Columbus discovered—or, in current parlance, "encountered"—the New World: America. The present-day Dominican Republic was one of the islands that he visited on his epochal first voyage.

The discovery was one of the most transformative events in history. It enormously expanded man's vision and knowledge of the known world, gave Europe and Spain global influence, led to what we would today call cultural anthropology, helped finance the Industrial Revolution, and served as the breakpoint between the medieval and modern worlds. It also led to a decimation of the indigenous population, produced slavery and the slave trade, gave rise to colonialism and imperialism, and shackled Latin America with a set of authoritarian, neoscholastic institutions that the area is only now beginning to overcome.

In 1992, we commemorate the five hundredth anniversary, the quincentennial, of the discovery. Major celebrations are planned in Spain, Italy, Latin America, and the United States. The Dominican Republic, as the first permanent Spanish colony in the New World, will also be celebrating with visits from the pope and the king of Spain, the construction of the Columbus lighthouse, the refurbishing of numerous parks and other historical monuments, and a general spiffing up of the capital city of Santo Domingo in anticipation of a major tourist influx.

The Dominican Republic, as this book makes clear, has had many "firsts." Not only was it the first permanent colony in the New World, it was also the site of the first cathedral, the first university, and the first monastery in the Americas. It was, additionally, where Spain's first colonial social, economic, and political experiments took place: the *encomienda* and *repartimiento* systems of exploiting native labor, the structure of hierarchical political authority, the complex patterns of social and race relations, and the mercantilist economic system. In moving toward its great national goals of development and democratization, the Dominican Republic is still trying to overcome this pervasive Hispanic colonial legacy.

When we wrote the first edition of this book in 1982, we used the concept of the "crucible" in our subtitle to indicate not only the Dominican Republic's historically important role in the Spanish empire but also the country's continuing importance as a crossroads of international conflict in the Caribbean and as an innovator in modernizing change and conflict. For it is in "the DR," as the nation is fondly referred to by those who have traveled and worked there, that some of the Western Hemisphere's earliest and most significant experiences with corporatism, bureaucratic-authoritarianism, developmentalism, dependency, interventionism, and now democratization have taken place. All the great issues of modern Latin America have been forged or are present in the DR. Hence, we see no reason to change the crucible metaphor; indeed, that image is now even more appropriate to any description of the Dominican Republic.

This second edition has been thoroughly revised and updated. It is, in this sense, a new book. But as we now reread our earlier words, the conclusions we reach are very much in keeping with the conclusions of the earlier edition. The Dominican Republic is still searching for its unique identity—its place in the sun—and although it has made great strides, much remains to be done.

Howard J. Wiarda
Michael J. Kryzanek

Acronyms
and Abbreviations

AID	Agency for International Development
CARICOM	Caribbean Economic Community
CDE	Dominican Electric Power Corporation
CEA	National Sugar Council
CEDOPEX	Dominican Center for the Promotion of Exports
CFI	Industrial Development Corporation
FED	Dominican Student Federation
FIDE	Investment Fund for Economic Development
GDP	gross domestic product
IAD	Dominican Agrarian Institute
IADB	Inter-American Development Bank
IAPF	Inter-American Peace Force
IDECOOP	Institute for Cooperative Development and Credit
ILO	International Labor Organisation
INDOTEC	Dominican Institute of Industrial Technology
INESPRE	Price Stabilization Institute
INFRATUR	Department of Tourist Investment and Infrastructure
JACC	Joint Agribusiness Coinvestment Council
LAFTA	Latin American Free Trade Association
MPD	Dominican Popular Movement
OAS	Organization of American States
ODC	Office of Community Development
OPEC	Organization of Petroleum Exporting Countries
OPIC	Overseas Private Investment Corporation
PCD	Dominican Communist Party
PLD	Dominican Liberation Party

PQD   Democratic Quisqueyan Party
PR   Reformist Party
PRD   Dominican Revolutionary Party
PRSC   Social Christian Reformist Party
UASD   Autonomous University of Santo Domingo
UCN   National Civic Union
UN   United Nations

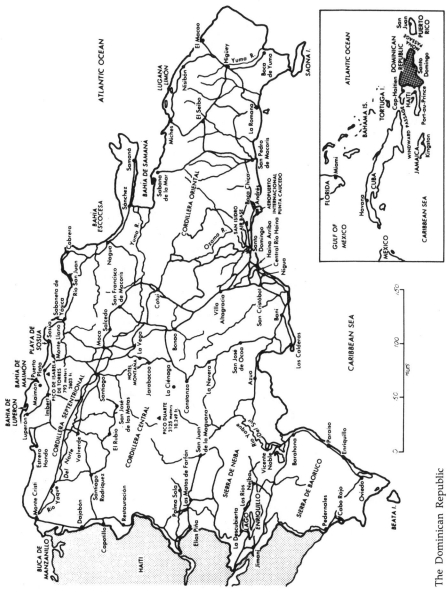

The Dominican Republic

1

Introduction

The importance of the Dominican Republic as a significant and influential member of the Latin American community of nations has seldom been recognized. Attention ebbs and flows, but most of it has been devoted to the larger and more populous countries of the area: those that are oil-rich or whose revolutions make dramatic headlines. The Dominican Republic, barely the size of South Carolina and with a population of approximately seven million, has frequently been overshadowed by countries whose natural resources, demographic figures, or internal politics put them in the spotlight of international attention.

The Dominican Republic may not hold the answer to the "mystery" of Latin America. Nor can it always compete for attention and notoriety with Argentina, Brazil, Chile, Cuba, or Mexico. Nevertheless, the Dominican Republic is an important nation, strategically located in the vortex of the Caribbean hurricane, a weather vane and direction pointer within the area. Dominican intellectual and former president Juan Bosch has written a book discussing the Caribbean as an "imperial frontier" during the past five hundred years, with the Dominican Republic at its center; and at least since the time of President James Polk, the United States has been interested in the strategic importance of the island, paying close attention to both its international connections and its internal politics. And, as stated in our preface, the Dominican Republic has had virtually everything the student of Latin American affairs might look for: great drama, conflict, and change.

The Dominican Republic is, in many respects, a microcosm of the entire area. Within this small nation's borders and throughout its history, it is possible to see all the wrenching divisions, developmental dilemmas, crises, and controversies characteristic of Latin America. The country has endured repeated interventions by foreign powers; those by the United States, from 1916 to 1924 and 1965 to 1966, are only the most recent. It continues to balance precariously between its strongly authoritarian traditions on the one hand and its democratic tradition on the other, now

1

complicated by the presence of various Socialist strains. It has to cope with the vicious circles of underdevelopment and the anxiety of a one-crop (sugar) dependent economy. It experiences the social upheavals and conflict precipitated by immense class differences and accelerated social change and the perpetual political tensions generated by the claims of rival elites who have largely incompatible views of how these problems should be met.

The Dominican Republic is not only a "central depository" of all that is Latin American, but it has also been a "living laboratory" for new social and political experiments. It has had its order-and-progress dictators, its periods of republican rule alternating with modernizing tyrannies, its eras of populism and change, a bloody revolution and civil war in 1965 that led to U.S. intervention, and a U.S.-sponsored recovery, and it is now adjusting to the challenges posed by a more open, competitive, and contentious democracy. In short, the Dominican Republic has often been a pacesetter for the rest of Latin America, both for good and for ill—a nation that has been a proving ground and, when the U.S. Marines landed, an alarm system. In the process, it has been the focus of numerous hemispheric conflicts in recent decades.

The Dominican Republic has frequently provided a fascinating pre-view of important shifts in the directions of Latin American political change and of U.S. policy toward the area. In 1905, the Dominican Republic provided the world with a first glimpse of the infamous Roosevelt Corol-lary to the Monroe Doctrine, under which the United States forcibly intervened in at least a half-dozen Latin American countries. In the regime of Rafael Trujillo, the Dominican Republic produced one of the world's longest-lived and most tightly knit dictatorships; his bloody rule increased our understanding of authoritarian and totalitarian control but was not very pleasant for many Dominicans. Trujillo's rule also provides an inter-esting case study of how the United States bolsters dictators who support its policies and then moves to undermine and, in this case, even assassinate them when they have outlived their usefulness.

For a time, the Dominican Republic was the showcase for the ill-fated U.S. aid program known as the Alliance for Progress. It was also in the Dominican Republic that the showcase shattered and the alliance collapsed—first when Juan Bosch's democratic government was over-thrown in 1963 and then definitively in 1965 when the United States sent its marines to crush a Bosch-led democratic revolution. The U.S. interven-tion there was a prelude to its even more massive intervention in Vietnam and signaled to the rest of Latin America that the United States would not permit revolutionary change in what it considered its sphere of influence. In 1978, however, the United States intervened again, this time diplomat-ically instead of militarily, to enable an elected Dominican social-democratic government to take power, rather than be overthrown by a military coup even before its inauguration. In the 1990s, the role of the United States in Dominican affairs has changed significantly. Due in large part to concern with instability and revolution in Central America and dwindling foreign aid dollars, Washington no longer views the Dominican Republic as a simmering security problem, as it did in the 1960s. The strengthening of democratic practice since 1978, coupled with growing interest in the country as a center of assembly plants, tourism, and agribusiness, has shifted Dominican attention toward trade, modernization, and economic reform. The Dominican Republic is not a hotbed of unrest nor a potential "second Cuba." Rather, in its relationship with the United States, the government of Joaquín Balaguer is mainly concerned with enhancing export opportunities, attracting investment, and renegotiating private and public debts.

The changeover from political tinderbox to anxious participant in economic development does not diminish the importance of the Dominican Republic as a beacon signaling the way of hemispheric changes in U.S.–Latin American relations. The initiatives taken by the Dominicans to make their country more attractive to foreign investors and their involvement in Caribbean trade places them in the forefront of the movement to reorganize the way in which this region deals with the outside world. As a result of innovative economic and political experiments, the Dominican Republic has enhanced its reputation as a frequent pacesetter in the hemisphere.

To introduce the Dominican Republic as innovator and bellwether and as having strategic significance beyond its size is to miss some other of its essential strengths, which makes it even more crucial that we give it our attention. The fact is that the Dominican Republic is a fascinating country in its own right. It has been struggling for five hundred years, against foreign occupiers and internal chaos, to establish its own institutional framework for development. Historically characterized by a lack of institutions—feudal or capitalist, conservative or liberal—the Dominican Republic has worked valiantly to fill this organizational void. Whether this effort will succeed, precisely what form its institutions will take, whether it is possible to blend outside influences and indigenous traditions—all these are still unknown. Only one thing is certain: The forms that are devised, the group and personal interrelations, the policy processes, and the habits of behavior and cultural patterns will be typically Dominican.

The profile of the Dominican Republic that is presented here will thus seek to explore the country from a number of vantage points. Chapter 2 will provide a general overview of the land, the culture, and the people, with special emphasis on the changing character of life in the Dominican Republic. Chapters 3 and 4 will describe the historical evolution of the country from the Spanish conquest to contemporary times. Chapters 5, 6, and 7 will be concerned, respectively, with the major social, economic, and political features of the country as well as the interrelationships of social class structure, economic dependency and underdevelopment, and political power. Chapters 8 and 9 will center on the key issues of policy and policymaking in both the domestic and the international arenas, focusing on the Dominican Republic's developmental options and its crucial relations with the United States.

Woven together throughout these chapters are a number of unifying threads and themes. These include an emphasis on the Dominican Republic's strategic and political importance and its position as a pacesetter, a microcosm, a *crucible* of Latin American social and political change. We shall insist on viewing the Dominican Republic in the light of its own history and cultural traditions, not from the frequently ethnocentric and biased viewpoint of the United States or Western Europe. We shall be concerned both with the nation's internal politics and economics and with its external dependency and interrelations with a broader world. Finally, we shall look sympathetically on the Dominican Republic's efforts to find its own place in the sun, to break out of its vicious circles of underdevelopment, to devise a more democratic political system—albeit democracy derived from its own traditions—to establish its position within a Caribbean region that is turbulent now and certain to become even more so in the near future.

Our study of the Dominican Republic seeks to weave these diverse themes together so the complete profile that is presented captures the distinctiveness of that country as well as its broader importance for understanding Caribbean, Latin American, and Third World contexts. We hope that the picture we draw will help others comprehend, with empathy and understanding, this land of beauty and misery, of richness and poverty, of hope and tragedy, of dreams lost and realized, and of abiding dignity, perseverance, and aspiration.

2

The Land, the People, the Culture

In 1492, when Columbus first sighted what is today the Dominican Republic, he reported to Spain that he had found a land that was "the fairest under the sun." Nestled in the chain of Caribbean islands between Cuba and Puerto Rico, the Dominican Republic, with its fertile valleys and plateaus, its favorable climate and gentle winds (except during hurricane season), its docile natives and considerable mineral wealth, was the favored early location for the seat of Spanish trade, culture, and administration in the New World. As proof of Columbus's love for the island and its importance in the early Spanish colonial empire, he named it "Española" (later Anglicized to "Hispaniola"), or "Little Spain."

THE LAND

The island of Hispaniola today is divided into two countries: the Dominican Republic, which is Hispanic, Western, Spanish-speaking, and predominantly white or mulatto; and Haiti, which is French and African culturally (though often with a thin veneer of Westernism), French- or *patois*-speaking (patois is a native dialect), and predominantly black. The Dominican Republic occupies the eastern two-thirds (19,386 square miles or 48,464 square kilometers) of Hispaniola, stretching from the mountainous regions in the north and west of the island to the eastern coast that looks out toward Puerto Rico. Haiti has about the same population in half as much territory. In history, culture, language, and racial attitudes, the two neighbors on Hispaniola have little in common. Nor, for the most part, have relations between them been friendly. The Dominicans believe the Haitians have an inferior culture and feel that those Haitians who enter the country should perform menial tasks such as cutting sugarcane. Increasingly, the Dominicans' negative perception of Haitians has led to acts of violence and calls for a lessening of Haitian emigration to the Dominican Republic.

The Haitian countryside is barren, impoverished, and largely denuded of vegetation, with most of its topsoil washed away. The Dominican Republic is lush and tropical, with rich vegetation. Travelers to the latter country consistently marvel at both the beauty and diversity of the topographical and climatic conditions. The Dominican countryside is a mixture of mountain ranges, semiarid deserts, rich farmlands, tropical rain forests, and picture-postcard beaches. Geographers who have studied the Dominican Republic call it one of the most diverse countries in the world, with over twenty distinct geographic regions.[1]

Dominating the central area of the country are the mountain ranges, or *cordilleras*. The Dominican Republic has four parallel mountain ranges running from northwest to southeast, chopping up the country into smaller segments and separating the capital city of Santo Domingo on the southern coast from the rich agricultural heartland in the Vega Real (the "Royal Plain") and from the center of the country's burgeoning tourist trade on the northern coast.

The mountain ranges, although majestic and beautiful, are largely unpopulated and are perhaps less important to the Dominican Republic than the valleys lying between these "fingers" of the cordillera. In the northern part of the country, surrounding the Dominican Republic's second largest city of Santiago, is the Cibão Valley. The Cibão is often referred to as the breadbasket of the country because of its production of grains, beef cattle, and export commodities such as tobacco.

Although the valleys of the northern cordilleras contain rich farming and grazing areas, the valleys in the southwest are semiarid deserts unsuitable to agriculture and with some of the poorest people to be found in the country. At the eastern end of the island, the cordillera gives way to a plain of over 1,000 square miles (2,590 square kilometers), much of it leased by multinational corporations such as Gulf and Western. It is a region of seemingly endless sugarcane fields, yielding the primary export commodity of the country. Surrounding the entire country are some of the loveliest and, until recently, most undeveloped beaches in the world.

The topographical diversity is reflected in considerable climatic diversity. The mountain areas are clear and cool, the plains and valleys warmer and more humid. But in general, the climate is temperate and more pleasant than in other tropical areas. The trade winds, high elevations, and surrounding ocean help keep the average temperature at 75 degrees year round. Rainfall is moderate except on the Samana Peninsula in the northeast part of the island and in the mountain areas around Santiago, where as much as 100 inches (254 centimeters) per year may

Cove in the Samaña Bay region (*courtesy of Judy Pinter*)

fall. The remainder of the country usually enjoys clear, sunny days with only an occasional afternoon or nighttime shower.

Although generally blessed with favorable temperatures and rainfall, the island has serious climatic problems as well. Hispaniola lies in the "hurricane channel." A killer hurricane devastated the capital in 1930, leaving thousands dead and many more thousands homeless, and served as a way by which Dominican dictator Rafael Trujillo justified even stronger authoritarian rule. In 1978, Hurricane David swept through the country killing more thousands and causing over $1 billion in damages— it was a storm from which the country still has not recovered. The Dominicans have also had to endure periodic droughts that have ruined the all-important sugar crop and caused severe water shortages, and they suffer almost yearly flooding, as poor drainage and river control systems have left certain areas constantly susceptible to the effects of excessive rainfall.

Despite the specter of hurricanes, droughts, and floods, climatic and topographical conditions are generally favorable to agriculture, which is still the backbone of the economy, the principal employer, and the chief source of export earnings. The Dominican Republic is one of the world's leading producers of sugar, a crop that shapes not only the nation's economy but also its sociology and politics. Although sugar continues to be a major generator of export earnings, its relative importance is diminishing. In fact, sugar export earnings have dropped 56 percent since 1983 as a result of a decline in world sugar prices and a reduction of about 75 percent in U.S. quotas. Coffee, tobacco, cocoa, bananas, tomatoes, and other fruits are also produced for export, but even these staple crops are facing declines. The Dominican government has sought to diversify traditional staple crops by working with foreign investors to develop nontraditional agricultural crops such as citrus fruits, pineapple, flowers, and winter fruits and vegetables. This change has helped to lessen the decline in the agricultural sector caused by shifts in investment toward other areas such as tourism and the assembly sector. Whereas in the past agriculture was the foundation of the Dominican economy, today it is one of a number of competing sectors.

The heavy dependence of the Dominicans on sugar and other staple crops in a world of unstable prices, however, has stimulated efforts at economic diversification, especially in the areas of mining and manufacturing. In recent years, the Dominican government has permitted foreign mining concerns to search for and extract for export bauxite, nickel, gypsum, gold, oil, and copper. The ferronickel industry near the city of Bonao has been especially successful and now provides nearly 15 percent of the government's revenues. The Dominican gold industry has also advanced quickly. With rising gold prices and a vast potential for mining and production, the Dominican Republic is fast becoming one of the world's leading suppliers of this precious metal.[2]

The effort to diversify the Dominican economy has also led to a major expansion of the tourist industry. Passed over for years by foreigners because of its unstable conditions, the Dominican Republic in the 1980s blossomed into one of the Caribbean's leading vacation spots. New hotels and tourist facilities are sprouting along the southern and northern coasts, and the government has pledged both funds and a major publicity campaign to attract tourists. The rationale behind this campaign is not just to bring sorely needed foreign currency into the country but also to stimulate employment. Tourism is labor-intensive, and in a nation that suffers from chronic unemployment and underemployment, tourism means money and jobs.

Business, commerce, and industry are also growing in the Dominican Republic. Over the past thirty years, as economic growth has accelerated, new industries (cement, plastics, textiles, construction, and a great variety of others) have been established, along with an increase in commerce, banking, and entrepreneurial activities. This has led to a greater diversification of the economy, a greater concentration of the wealth and power in Santo Domingo, and a country that is no longer a "sleepy banana (or sugar) republic" but rather one that is dynamic and fast-changing. Probably the most significant development in the Dominican economy is the presence of industrial free zones, which can be found throughout the country. Host to hundreds of foreign enterprises seeking low-cost labor and investment incentives, these industrial zones have become home to assembly plants that produce everything from apparel to semiconductors and employ thousands of eager Dominicans.

The changing character of the economy from predominantly agricultural to one increasingly more diversified has had a major impact on the country's demography. Today, for the first time, more people live in urban than in rural areas. The influx of people to the two largest cities, Santo Domingo and Santiago, has been immense. The population of the capital increased from 820,000 in 1970 to an estimated 2.4 million in 1990. Sizable increases have also occurred in such smaller cities as La Romana, Bonao, and Puerto Plata, reflecting their respective sugar, mining, and tourism booms. The overall population has climbed from 4 million in 1970 to over 7 million in 1990.

The influx of people to the cities has created new problems and tensions as the newcomers compete for jobs and insufficient housing, services, and essentials such as water. The shantytown *barrios* around Santo Domingo often have no electricity, no real streets, no running water, and no sewage facilities. Yet life in the city is still preferable to that in the impoverished countryside, so the urban migration continues.

George Washington Boulevard, Santo Domingo (*Warren Smith; courtesy of Public Affairs Analysts, Inc.*)

LIFE IN THE DOMINICAN CITY

Almost half the Dominican population still lives in the *campo* ("countryside"), often eking out a meager subsistence, living in huts made of mud, sticks, and thatch. Many work as peasants, tenants, or sharecroppers, cast with their families into a life of poverty, misery, illiteracy (about 40 percent of the population), and malnutrition. It is clear that the future lies elsewhere. To more and more Dominicans fleeing the wretched poverty of the campo, that future lies in the cities. Perhaps the changing society and demography of the Dominican Republic can be understood best by examining life in four representative cities: Santo Domingo, Santiago, La Romana, and Puerto Plata.

Santo Domingo

The capital of the country since 1496, when Bartholomew Columbus (Christopher's brother) founded it, Santo Domingo is, in nearly all respects,

Central market in Santo Domingo (*Warren Smith; courtesy of Public Affairs Analysts, Inc.*)

the center of the country. Not only is it the seat of national power and administration, but it is also the hub of financial and business activity, the chief location of the country's thriving middle class, the site of the largest institution of higher learning, and the center of cultural attractions that include art galleries, libraries, museums, and concert halls. Socially, politically, and financially, Santo Domingo is "where the action is," which explains its tremendous recent growth. If the Dominican Republic can be characterized as a city-state–sized nation, then Santo Domingo, the primary city, is its focal point.

Santo Domingo has a history unmatched by any other in Latin America. As Spain's first administrative capital in the New World, it was the site of the first hospital, first monastery, first cathedral, and first university. The city has survived devastating hurricanes, swashbuckling pirates, numerous foreign occupations, and destructive civil wars. Yet, centered on a promontory overlooking the blue Caribbean, it retains its beauty, dignity, and sense of history.

As with any capital city, Santo Domingo is alive with activity and reflects the changes in Dominican society and economics. The "old city," with its cobblestone streets, open-air markets, small shops, and craftsmen, is gradually giving way to new suburban housing and supermarkets on the outskirts of town. Construction is booming as Dominican and foreign interests recognize the importance of the capital as a business, industrial, and tourist center.[3]

Among the more exciting aspects of life in Santo Domingo for the visitor are the restoration efforts undertaken by the national government. Beginning in the early 1970s, large sections of the old city were tastefully restored to their colonial state. The cornerstone of this effort is the Alcazar de Colon, the first castle in the New World built by Columbus's son Diego.

Behind this facade of wealth and beauty, however, is the other face of Santo Domingo. The capital is also the home of hundreds of thousands of poor, unemployed, and increasingly desperate and angry people who have been bypassed by the new wealth and prosperity they see all around. The poor barrios of Santo Domingo serve as a stark reminder to all that the economic advances of the past decade are uneven and benefit but a small percentage of the total population. It is from these poor barrios that the "shock troops" for some future Dominican revolution will likely come.

Santiago

Overshadowed by the growth and dynamism of Santo Domingo is Santiago, the country's second largest city (once its largest). Often referred to by its full Spanish name of Santiago de los Caballeros ("Santiago of the Gentlemen"), this city of 400,000, in the heart of the Cibão Valley, has traditionally been recognized as the country's agricultural center. Santiago is home to a number of the nation's wealthy aristocrats and historic families and, as a result, has a reputation as a center of culture and refinement; local residents often prefer it to the brashness, noise, and materialism of Santo Domingo.

Although Santiago is a growing city and attracting new commercial and industrial concerns to complement its agricultural base, it continues to be defined in terms of a handful of key, closely interrelated families, who have controlled the politics and economics of both the region and the nation for generations. Family names with deep historical roots in Dominican history, like Cáceres, Espaillat, Grullón, Taváres, Cabral, and now Guzmán, are at the heart of the social oligarchy of Santiago.

Because of the influence of this aristocracy, politics in Santiago and its surrounding countryside have remained more traditional and conservative than in Santo Domingo. Separated by 100 miles from the capital's frenzy and sprawl, Santiago remains a city of relative quiet and serenity. In many respects, it is an important counterforce to the political, social, and economic climate of Santo Domingo. While Santo Domingo is alive with the dynamics of capitalism, boom times, and class and partisan conflict, Santiago remains almost feudal in its age-old relationships— more tranquil, stable, traditional.

La Romana

La Romana, a provincial capital, is probably the best example of a medium-sized city that mirrors the changes in the Dominican economy. Situated on the southern coast toward the eastern end of the island, La Romana has been the center of the country's sugar industry, a leading resort area (site of the famed Casa del Campo), and a model of transition from the old economy to the new.

La Romana received attention during the postrevolutionary period because it was so directly affected by multinational control of the Dominican Republic's most precious resource—sugar. The U.S. conglomerate Gulf and Western came to La Romana in the early 1960s and invested heavily in sugar refining, tourism, cattle, cement, and real estate. At the peak of its involvement, Gulf and Western had invested over $200 million in and around La Romana, creating both excitement and suspicion. To show its goodwill, the multinational spent an estimated $20 million in making the city "the showcase of the East." Schools, churches, clinics, parks, recreation centers, and employee housing were built.

There was, however, a dark side to the showcase. To run its operation, Gulf and Western employed tough and brutal administrators who often bribed Dominican politicians to get their way, paid off local police and

military commanders to intimidate leftist party activists and union organizers, and created a classic company town atmosphere that weakened
any attempt at independence or control. But as the Dominican Republic
shifted from authoritarianism to democracy in 1978 and the price of sugar
and the level of U.S. quotas sank, Gulf and Western tired of its investment.
A change of leadership at the multinational spelled the end of what had
become one of the more notorious examples of U.S. business involvement
in Latin America. Gulf and Western sold its sugar interests to the Fanjul
family of Miami and quietly left La Romana.

Since the departure of Gulf and Western, La Romana has become
enmeshed in the transition to a new economy. In 1986, the government
sugar enterprise, the National Sugar Council (CEA), entered into a joint
venture with the Dole Company to develop 4,000 acres of sugar plantation
for pineapple exportation. The development of the pineapple lands is but
the first step in changing La Romana's image from a sugar town. New
tourist investment is finding its way into the region, along with industrial
free zones. Moreover, the Dominican government is clearly seeking to de-
emphasize sugar by cutting back the work force and reducing public
investment. As a result, La Romana is gradually losing its reputation as a
sugar town and instead becoming known as a diversified center of industry
and tourism. For many of the city's residents, the shift has brought new
life to their town and new hope for a more vibrant and less dependent
economy.

Puerto Plata

Perhaps no city more accurately reflects the changing character of
the Dominican economy than Puerto Plata. Situated on the rapidly developing north coast, the city has become a symbol of the burgeoning tourist
sector in the Dominican Republic. Once a quiet coastal hamlet, Puerto
Plata is now the center of the hotel and resort boom that has made the
country the top tourist attraction in the Caribbean, offering more rooms
than the Bahamas, Jamaica, and Puerto Rico. Furthermore, the emphasis
that the Dominican government has placed on tourism has had an enormous spillover effect in the Puerto Plata area. A privately built and publicly
run international airport, new roads, water facilities, sewer systems, and,
most importantly, jobs have made Puerto Plata a mecca not only for
foreigners anxious to relax on pristine beaches but for Dominicans seeking
employment in the hotel and ancillary services industries.

Although Puerto Plata is the center of north coast development, the
rush to transform this region into an international tourist attraction has
also had a positive impact on surrounding towns. Sosua, once known
primarily for its Jewish settlements, has become the site of a number of

Typical house in Puerto Plata (*courtesy of the Dominican Republic Tourism Promotion Council*)

condominium projects and single-family villas. Further east from Puerto Plata and Sosua are the newly developing resort regions of Playa Grande, Playa Dorada, and Cabarete. Pelican Resort and Casino recently announced that it would build a $50-million, all-suite resort in Cabarete, reinforcing the ongoing development of the region in and around Puerto Plata. With dizzying regularity, investors from the United States, Canada, and Europe continue to announce new tourist ventures and added development of Puerto Plata.

In the past, tourists arriving in the Dominican Republic typically chose Santo Domingo with its rich colonial heritage and its big-city hustle and bustle. Today, however, many tourists land at Puerto Plata International Airport, enjoy the recreation the area has to offer, and then board a plane out of the Dominican Republic without setting foot in the capital city. Just as the Dominican economy has become more diversified, so too have the centers of economic activity. Santo Domingo must now compete with Puerto Plata for the ever-growing tourist dollar, a competition that can only strengthen the Dominican economy.

THE DOMINICAN PEOPLE AND THEIR CULTURE

To describe the Dominican Republic only in terms of its geography, landscape, resources, and demography is to ignore some essential ingredients. As with any country, it is the people—their social and racial patterns, their ethnic heritage, and their religious beliefs, language pat-

Carnival mask from La Vega (*courtesy of Suzanne Murphy*)

terns, personality profile, and behaviors—in short, their culture—that forms the foundation for national identity.

Unlike many of the Latin American nations, the Dominican Republic is relatively homogeneous in terms of its racial composition. The native Indian population was quickly decimated by conquest, forced labor, and the diseases carried by the Spaniards for which the Indians had no immunity. Within fifty years of the Spanish colonization, the native population and culture had been almost completely eliminated.[4]

The Spaniards brought in African labor to replace the Indians in the mines and on the plantations. Over time, a complex racial melting pot was formed, in which the mulatto became the dominant element numerically. Today, nearly two-thirds of the Dominican population is officially listed as mulatto. Within that category, numerous subtle shadings and subcategories are used by the Dominicans.

Although the mulatto is most numerous, the country has historically been led by its white, Hispanic elements. Whites dominate business, finance, the prestigious professions, government, and high society. Mulatto elements are preponderant in the military officer corps, the provincial towns, the less prestigious professions, and among lower- to middle-level government officials.

Race and class are closely tied together. The white element tends to be wealthier and to form the Dominican elite. The middle classes tend to be mulatto. The working classes, rural and urban, tend to be black or dark mulatto. Despite the claims of some Dominicans to the contrary, racism is present in the Dominican Republic, and there is no doubt that, as one moves up the social scale, race is a very important factor separating social classes and economic positions. In comparison with the United States, there is relatively little manifest racial prejudice in the Dominican Republic, seldom an expression of racial hatred among Dominican nationals, and little segregation along strictly racial lines. But recent incidents of racial violence between Dominicans and Haitians who have settled in the country have forced many to reevaluate the whole issue of race relations.[5]

In addition to these dominant racial categories, there are small pockets of other ethnic and nationality groups in the Dominican Republic. The important business and financial community of Santo Domingo contains a considerable number of Lebanese members. Many of the finest restaurants in the capital are owned by Chinese. A number of Italian and French families have gained influence. A few Jewish families remain, of the hundred or so who came as refugees during the period of the Holocaust. There is a community of Japanese farmers and, of course, a large community of Americans. Many Haitians and West Indians, brought in during the cane-cutting season, have stayed within Dominican borders.

Although there is considerable diversity in the country's racial and ethnic makeup, language and religion are a different story. Because of the absence of a native Indian population and the dominance of the Spanish tradition, the Dominican Republic is almost exclusively a Spanish-speaking nation. There are some regional dialects, but Spanish is *the* language of the country. Moreover, Dominican Spanish is a very clear, almost classical Spanish, in keeping with the Dominicans' pride in being the first settled colony and having the "purest" Spanish traditions in Latin America.

The proximity to North America and the powerful influence of the United States in the Dominican Republic has led to some "coca-colaization" of the language and culture. Baseball is the national sport, and U.S. music and styles are widespread. "Home-run" is almost the same whether rendered in English or Spanish. Furthermore, the movement of Dominicans from their native land to the United States, particularly New York City, and the growing interest in the country by U.S. investors have increased the use of English. At present, it is common for many Dominican businesspeople to speak English and for those so-called Dom Yorks who have spent some time in the United States to take pride in their bilingual facility and their knowledge of U.S. life and culture.

The dominance of the Spanish language is matched by the centrality of the Catholic church and Catholic beliefs and culture. Approximately 98 percent of the Dominican population is Catholic. As with many nations, this figure does not represent actual participation in church sacraments, but it does reflect the importance and pervasiveness of the country's Catholicism.

The Dominican Catholic church prides itself on its strong historical roots dating back to Columbus, its defense of the hapless Indians, and its contributions to Dominican culture and society. For a long time, the Dominican hierarchy had a reputation for conservatism and unwillingness to become involved in matters of social justice and political repression. At two critical junctures in Dominican history, during the Trujillo dictatorship (1930–1961) and in the 1965 revolution, the church was seen as playing an overly passive and conservative role while many Dominicans were suffering.

The church nonetheless remains a strong and vital part of the Dominican society. Its influence is major in the areas of education and health, as well as religion. On some political issues (family planning, divorce, even the choice of a president), the church's voice can be powerful. The past prominence as well as present dilemmas of the church in the Dominican Republic were recognized by Pope John Paul II, who has singled out this nation as an essential stop on a number of his tours of Latin America. He further acknowledged the importance of the church in the Dominican Republic by naming Nicolás de Jésus López Rodríguez, the archbishop of Santo Domingo, as cardinal in 1991. Yet, despite the importance of the Dominican Catholic church to Rome and the pride expressed by the Dominican people toward their church leaders, Protestant evangelical movements have made significant inroads in the spiritual life of the country. Faced with a lack of funds, priests, and social programs attractive to the people, the Catholic church has seen its base of support challenged by aggressive Protestant ministries whose accent on biblical fundamentalism and personal and familial rejuvenation, together with a strong dose of economic entrepreneurship, has taken hold in the country and also in the storefront churches of New York City. Although the Catholic

Young Dominican baseball players (*courtesy of the Dominican Republic Tourism Promotion Council*)

church continues to be the dominant religious institution in the country, there is now competition from a vocal and active minority.

The hardest task in describing a nation other than one's own is to define precisely its special character and culture without falling into the dangers of oversimplification and stereotyping. There are always exceptions, of course, and making generalizations about a country's unique or dominant behavior can be dangerous. We need to keep these limitations in mind, but it is also useful to try to understand those cultural patterns that appear constant in Dominican society.

As in many of the Latin American nations, one is initially struck in the Dominican Republic by the male dominance and the sense of *machismo* that males display. The outward concern to appear strong and domineering, the prideful prance when others are looking, the sexual comments to passing females, the camaraderie among males, and the double standard that applies in the relations of husbands, wives, and mistresses are but a few of the manifestations of an underlying need to appear superior and in control, sexually and otherwise. Male children are coddled, spoiled, and not disciplined; certainly, this early experience is reflected in their later social and political behavior.

Machismo also helps explain why power is in the hands of males while women are expected to be docile, protected, and submissive. More and more Dominican women are working, however, joining the professions and playing an increasing role in politics (President Joaquín Balaguer named women to serve as governors of all the nation's provinces); the Dominican women's movement is still weak, but change is clearly in the air. Furthermore, evidence is accumulating that, although the male is the strong partner outside the home, the woman is dominant within the home, managing the family and controlling the purse strings.

If the machismo of Dominican males is readily observable, so too is the friendliness and expressiveness of the people. Despite their history of misfortune, the people of the Dominican Republic have a well-deserved reputation for goodwill and personal warmth. Dominicans are cordial in greeting, patient and expressive in conversation, and gracious in parting. On a larger scale, Dominicans reveal a sense of joy and passion that makes for a society of street-corner singing, fiercely dedicated baseball fans, and explosive political demonstrations.

Beneath these outward expressions of gaiety, friendliness, politeness, and passion, there is a noticeable strain of quiet resignation—but also perseverance. Surprisingly, the suffering that Dominicans have endured historically from both domestic tyrants and foreign oppressors has registered not so much in the form of anger or bitterness (although there are those who display such feelings) as in a fatalistic acceptance of their lot and a desire to return to normalcy. Dominicans have a clear vision of a better tomorrow, but experience has led them to be reluctant to take risks to achieve their hopes. After centuries of neglect, backwardness, wars, repression, dictatorship, underdevelopment, intervention, and hurricanes, such resignation should not be too surprising.

This history also lies at the heart of Dominican political attitudes, particularly the lingering influence of Trujillo and his system of dominance, authority, and control. Although Trujillo was assassinated in 1961, his memory, style, and system survive.

Although many Dominicans express outward hatred of Trujillo, they tend to admire him secretly for his strength, showmanship, and national accomplishments. Trujillo and Trujilloism are constant topics of conversation in the Dominican Republic for the leader was a *caudillo*, a man on horseback, a macho authority figure par excellence, and much of what can be described as sociopolitical analysis in the country still begins and almost literally ends with Trujillo. Evaluations of the success or failure of virtually any regime in recent Dominican history almost always use Trujillo as the measuring rod, for good or ill.

Dominicans seem to have a love-hate relationship with Trujillo. They hated his bloody terror, the stifling censorship, the torture and secret police. But they admire his economic accomplishments, his machismo, the attention he brought the country, the "show" he put on, and his ability to impose order and organization on an unruly country. As one prominent Dominican put it, "There is a little of Trujillo in all of us."[6]

Trujillo has been gone now for over thirty years, but Dominicans continue to see his influence on the body politic. His heirs and followers are still active: Joaquín Balaguer, president from 1966 to 1978 and from 1986 to the present, clearly modeled his regime on that of Trujillo (but without the terror), and Trujillo's popularity remains strong, especially in times of national breakdown and chaos (which occur frequently in the Dominican Republic). The sense of order and discipline he provided, the economic development he helped usher in, and his personal involvement in the lives of his subjects are all attractive to Dominicans—all the more so because those features have been so rare in Dominican history. Many have sought to suppress or repudiate the things that Trujillo stood for, but that is hard because these traits are so strongly Dominican and the Trujillo regime was so much a reflection of Dominican society and values.

Trujilloism seems to be a system of values and institutions that Dominicans publicly disavow but privately uphold. Liberal democracy is also a recurring theme, a system that many Dominicans would like to see established but that they seem unwilling or unable to achieve. Dominican history is full of numerous but largely unsuccessful efforts to establish a democratic system. Thus, although Dominicans admire democracy in the abstract, they are often skeptical of whether it can work in their country, given its disorder and lack of organization, and they often secretly prefer the authority and unity of strongman rule.

The repeated failures of democracy and democratic governments have not, however, curtailed the commitment of many Dominicans to achieve democracy and constitutionalism. Throughout their nation's long history of dictatorial rule, the passion of Dominicans for democracy did not falter but grew stronger. Some of the most influential democratic movements grew most rapidly during the periods of strongest authoritarian rule. In fact, the election of Joaquín Balaguer in 1986 and his reelection in 1990 can be viewed as a significant victory of democracy over authoritarian rule. In his previous administrations from 1966–1978, Balaguer tolerated repression within the ranks of the military and the national police and often ignored the institutional structures of a constitutional democracy. Now, however, he has accepted and built on the social democracy introduced by presidents Antonio Guzmán and Jorge Blanco. Balaguer is, in many respects, a reformed authoritarian who, although still enamored of central rule and personalism, has yielded to the pressure for a more open and plural policymaking process.

Nevertheless, despite the current era of democratic reform, the passion for democracy so strongly present in Dominican politics exists alongside the desire for unified, disciplined, authoritarian rule. These two traditions, the one democratic and the other authoritarian, run parallel in the national history. The country is caught between these two conflicting visions. The Dominicans would like to have democracy, but they are somewhat fearful of its consequences and uncomfortable with the disorder, the license, the potential for chaos that this implies. They also admire discipline and order, but they do not want the oppressive tyranny into which this all too often degenerates. So far, they have not found a proper formula for blending or reconciling these opposing currents that run so strongly throughout their life.[7]

We should mention, finally, the way Dominican political culture has been influenced by its multifaceted relationship with the United States. That too is a mix of love and hate. In few countries has the U.S. presence been so strong or so persistent over such a long time. That presence has brought economic development and a measure of protection to the Dominicans, but it has also brought exploitation and unwarranted interference in internal Dominican affairs.

U.S. influence is political, military, economic, and cultural, and it affects all areas of Dominican life. Perhaps its most interesting effects can be seen in the attitudes of the Dominican people. Americans who visit the country often marvel at the kind reception they receive from the people. Outwardly, most Dominicans express fondness for the United

States and the American way of life; there is little manifest anti-Americanism.

These appearances, however, cannot mask the ambivalence many
Dominicans feel, the suspicion and mistrust many of them have but are
too polite to express. Most Dominicans are too pragmatic to be carried
away by the rhetoric of the anti-Yankee hatemongers present in the
country, but they know enough of past Dominican history to view U.S.
political leaders, corporate administrators, and embassy personnel with
some apprehension. They are respectful and often cooperative, but they
seek to keep their distance. Americans bring in tourist dollars, new
technology, and foreign aid, but Dominicans know there is a price to be
paid in terms of loss of sovereignty, dependence on the "colossus of the
north," and the Americanization of their culture.

What is astounding is not this wariness but that the history of
repeated U.S. intervention and manipulation has not completely soured
Dominican-U.S. relations. After all, it was not long ago (1965) that U.S.
troops occupied the Dominican Republic and were shooting at Dominicans
they erroneously assumed to be Castro-Communists. It is a testament to
the Dominicans' patience, stoicism, and capacity to forgive that they have
not become virulently anti-American but rather have chosen to cooperate
with a neighbor that historically has treated their country as if it were a
satellite and not a sovereign nation.

*   *   *

The simple little island paradise that Columbus sighted in 1492 has
since become a complex and diversified nation. Its aspirations include
economic growth and independence, a more equitable distribution of
income, political stability and democracy, a small but dignified place in
the Caribbean sun. These are modest goals, but they have been thwarted
repeatedly by domestic politics, by internal social and class rigidities, and
by the international contingencies over which the Dominicans have no
control.

These forces have served to retard the nation's development, and
coupled with an incredible and often bizarre history, a complex racial
melting pot, some major distortions in the economy, and conflicting
cultural traditions, they have left the Dominican Republic a country of
contradictions. Unable to break with a past that is authoritarian, elitist,
and semifeudal, its destiny shaped as often by foreign conquests and
intervention as by domestic needs, mired in enormous social and economic
problems, and unable to devise a political formula for development that
resolves its various contradictions, the Dominican Republic represents an
uneasy joining together of tradition and modernity, conflict and stability,
wealth and poverty, idealism and cynicism.

To some, these contradictions reinforce the notion that the Dominican Republic is just another Third World country struggling to overcome its past. To the Dominicans, however, these contradictions reveal the essence of their heritage and their challenge for the future—their desire to resolve or live with their problems on their own terms and to devise a uniquely Dominican developmental formula, rather than some pale and retarded imitation of the already developed nations. As we move forward and examine the course of the Dominican Republic's history, its social and economic structure and relations, and the nature of its political system, we will consider how this nation will be able to deal with these wrenching contradictions in its national life.

3

The Pattern of
Historical Development

The course of Dominican history is intricate, often chaotic, sometimes regressive, consistently fascinating. It is not a history of gradual, evolutionary, and inevitable progress toward some agreed on goal or a national "manifest destiny." Rather, Dominican history consists of starts and stops, forward surges and throwbacks to earlier and simpler eras, great turmoil and ruinous foreign interventions, slow and gradual change that is then thwarted by domestic tyrants, natural disasters, and unfinished and frustrated revolutions. Throughout the course of this history, some common themes appear and reappear, shaping this unique and often unfortunate legacy.

THE COLONIAL ERA

To properly understand Dominican history, we must go back not just to the nation's declaration of independence but to the colonial era, to the powerful legacy implanted by Spain on Hispaniola.

The discovery of the island by Columbus in 1492 was a major historical event, the beginning of a process by which European civilization was spread to the far-flung corners of the globe. Spain was the first great colonial power, and Latin America was the first of the non-Western areas to be drawn into the European orbit.

The Spanish decision to found Santo Domingo as its initial capital in the New World was, at best, a mixed blessing. For a time, the colony flourished as a center of transplanted European culture. A walled enclave city grew up patterned after those of medieval Spain; churches were erected, schools and hospitals built, and commerce, agriculture, and mining flourished. But the native Indians were quickly decimated, black slavery was introduced, and a rigid two-class system, reinforced by racial criteria, was established.[1]

The "civilizing" process undertaken by Spain was incomplete and short-lived. After the first fifty years, the more enterprising Spaniards moved on to other islands or to the mainland, where there was more gold and silver and more Indians to enslave. The Spaniards apparently had a greater interest in enriching themselves than in developing their New World colonies. The island of Hispaniola was an early victim of this exploitative, get-rich-quick philosophy. Once its native labor supply had been depleted and its readily available mineral wealth exhausted, it was quickly abandoned.

Although the *conquistadores* sailed off to Cuba, Mexico, and other territories, they left behind a powerful colonial legacy and a vision of a "golden age." The system of two-class social relations, of political author-itarianism and hierarchy, of a centralized and state-dominated economy and society, and of political and religious unity had been strongly im-planted on Hispaniola. Moreover, because these institutions were associ-ated with the glory and prosperity of Hispaniola in its first fifty years, they continued to represent an ideal model to which subsequent Domini-can regimes would aspire. The Spanish may have abandoned Santo Domingo, but they left their mark indelibly stamped on the society. In the establishment and remarkable perseverance of these institutions, the Dominican Republic can be viewed as both the first and the most typical Latin American state.

The diversion of colonial attention from Hispaniola to Mexico and elsewhere left the once-proud and important outpost in a sad state of neglect. Hispaniola became an underpopulated, undeveloped, and forgot-ten colony that offered little to the mother country or even to passing pirates. Its previously flourishing mines and plantations were abandoned, the economy reverted to a more primitive subsistence state, and the city of Santo Domingo fell into a bedraggled condition. What trade existed was primarily in cowhides for the staple commodities like sugar, cotton, and tobacco that would later make the economy grow again were not properly managed or developed. The island was socially, politically, and economically disorganized and unorganized.

For over two hundred years, the colony remained in this depressed condition, hopelessly thrust into the back pages of the Spanish colonial empire. Weak and underdeveloped, no longer of interest to the Spanish crown, it eventually became, as the Caribbean itself became, an imperial frontier for the rivalries among that era's superpowers, a pawn to be bartered between them. In the late 1500s and throughout the seventeenth century, the French, Spanish, and British competed for control of the island. Dutch pirates also sought a foothold. Despite the opposition of the English, Spain ceded the western one-third of the island to the French in 1697. Nearly one hundred years later, although the Spanish part of the island had experienced a mild resurgence, the Madrid government was no longer able or willing to administer such a vast colonial empire. In 1795, the Spanish ceded the eastern two-thirds to France as well.

The contrasts between the French-controlled section of Hispaniola (by that time called Hayti) and the former Spanish colony were pronounced. By 1790, the French colony contained 520,000 people and, based on black slavery, was a prospering colony producing sugar and cotton. Indeed, among all the colonial possessions in the world at that time, Hayti was the most prosperous; at one time, England gave serious thought to bartering its thirteen colonies in North America for Hayti!

On the other hand, in the larger Spanish-speaking territory on Hispaniola, there were less than 100,000 people living on a meager subsistence or from contraband trade in meat and hides with Hayti. Those who could afford to leave continued to abandon the colony for a better life elsewhere. What was left behind can only be described as the rundown remnant of Spanish administration and culture.

The granting of the eastern two-thirds of Hispaniola to France in 1795 brought no relief. In fact, the opposite occurred: The colony slid further downhill. The shift in control from Spain to France introduced a half century of repeated foreign intervention, maladministration, racial conflict, and ruination. The spark that ignited the blaze was the slave revolt in Hayti. Led by slave revolutionaries Toussaint L'Ouverture and Henry Dessalines, the rebels succeeded in establishing in Hayti (now spelled Haiti) the world's first black republic.[2]

After defeating the French, the black armies moved eastward into the former Spanish colony. From 1804 to 1809, the Haitians, French, and Spanish fought to determine who would eventually control the entire island. The British, who had economic and imperial designs of their own, aided the Spanish in driving the Haitians back to the west. From 1809 to 1821, the eastern colony was restored to Spanish administration.

The vulnerability of the colony to the whims of colonial masters and expansionist neighbors was made clear once more in 1821. The Spanish had again bungled as colonial administrators, and the Dominicans had, along with the other Latin American territories, declared their independence. Within weeks, however, Haitian armies had again overrun the entire island. Under their military leader, Jean Pierre Boyer, the Haitians swept across Hispaniola, leaving a trail of blood and destruction. This Haitian occupation, 1822–1844, is often viewed as the initial cause of the racial, social, and political antagonism that even today separates Dominicans from Haitians. However, there were also some positive elements in the occupation, particularly the freeing of the slaves.

The Dominicans continued to view the Haitians as interlopers more interested in plunder than effective administration, and soon sentiment

Independence Park, with part of the ancient city wall, Santo Domingo (*courtesy of Milton T. Cole*)

for independence grew. The leader of the independence movement was a philosopher, visionary, and literary romantic named Juan Pablo Duarte. Although most of Latin America's great liberators had since left the scene, Duarte had not forgotten their impassioned cries for democracy and independence. He and his associates formed a secret society, "La Trinitaria," that led the independence movement.

THE INDEPENDENCE ERA

By 1844, the Haitian hold on the increasingly nationalistic Dominicans was waning. An earthquake that struck in 1842, destroying numerous Dominican cities, had helped catalyze the opposition. Haiti itself was torn by domestic rivalries and civil war. With financial backing from Venezuela, Duarte and his fellow conspirators attacked the Haitian garrisons in a surprise move that led to a largely bloodless revolt. In 1844, he entered Santo Domingo triumphant, and the Dominican Republic was declared an independent nation.

The father of Dominican independence, however, was reluctant to wield the levers of power. While Duarte procrastinated and was soon exiled, political power was consolidated in the hands of two self-appointed generals, Buenaventura Báez and Pedro Santana. These two men soon stepped into the vacuum left by Duarte. Santana marched on the capital and declared himself dictator.

The rise to power of Santana and his "partner" in national leadership, Báez, ushered in what historians call the "era of the dual caudillos." For the next forty-five years, these two "men on horseback" dominated Dominican politics, ruling directly or through compliant puppets. Santana and Báez alternated in the presidency and used their positions to enrich themselves at public expense.[3]

Although it is difficult to decipher the national objectives of these two dictators, both had a vague design to restore the country to its earlier order and greatness and to develop close ties with a foreign protector. Both sought, unsuccessfully, to restore the sixteenth-century colonial model, complete with the protection of a benevolent large power. Both feared the continuous invasions of a more populous Haiti, and they approached, in turn, England, France, Spain, and the United States to offer an alliance and concessions as a way of safeguarding the country from invasion. The protectorate idea and the concessions, however, also made the Dominican Republic a dependency—sometimes a virtual colony—of these larger powers.

The Dominican Republic managed to hold off the Haitians and keep the larger nations at arm's length for a time, but by 1861, the country was bankrupt as a result of corruption, maladministration, disastrous trade policies, and the constant need to repel Haiti's thrusts. Santana, now president for the third time, announced that the country would be reincorporated as a Spanish colony. By midsummer 1861, Santo Domingo was full of Spanish soldiers, officials, and priests who reintroduced the Spanish monopoly system of trade and administration. By midfall, the Dominicans had already organized a revolt against Spanish rule. The nationalistic revolt also served to discredit Santana, who died in disgrace in 1864. Báez, however, still had many years left at the center of national politics.

With Santana out of the picture and Spain unable to maintain its hold, the new independence movement led by Gregorio Luperón met with scant resistance. The departure of the Spanish in 1865 opened up a new era of hope for Dominicans seeking lasting independence and the restoration of democratic government. Unfortunately, as before, poor leadership, divisions among the elite, and foreign intrigue helped stymie these hopes.

In 1865, Báez was inaugurated president for the third time, but his ascension to power immediately precipitated a rebellion led by General Luperón. Forced to leave after only five months in office, Báez remained "on call," confident that his successors would fail. He was right.

In the midst of this "revolving door" brand of politics, Báez returned to power again in 1866 and promptly set about trying to negotiate loans and lease arrangements with several foreign powers (Britain, France, the United States) that were designed to extricate the country from its mounting indebtedness. Like Santana, Báez sought a foreign protector and even tried to convince the Grant administration of the wisdom of annexing the Dominican Republic to the United States. The move failed by only one vote when the Senate acted on the related treaty. These efforts to sell the country to the highest bidder touched off renewed rebellion and toppled Báez from power for the fourth time.

The years 1874–1879 were again marked by hope and promise as a reform president, Ulises Espaillat, came to power on the heels of Báez's overthrow. He promised to administer the nation's finances honestly and to govern constitutionally. Espaillat was in the tradition of Duarte, long on ideals but weak on practical realities. He proved unable to manage the contentious forces in the nation and soon fell from power. Báez returned again.

The fifth presidency of Báez was his shortest. Rebellion against him broke out immediately, and he fell in two months—but not before pilfering $300,000 from the treasury and fleeing to Puerto Rico. In his wake, Báez left a country bankrupt, factionalized, still dependent on foreign powers, and without any training in democratic self-government. While many Latin American countries were by this time consolidating their leaderships and developing economic stability, the Dominican Republic was still picking up the pieces of a chaotic and depressed economy and a society anxious for relief from caudillo rule.

The political and economic disruptions occasioned by nearly a hundred years of repeated international traumas, Haitian occupations, and ruinous caudilloism came to an abrupt halt with the coming to power in 1882 of a modernizing dictator, Ulises Heureaux. For the next seventeen years, Heureaux ran a tightly knit regime, again patterned on the "glorious" sixteenth-century Spanish model, that combined vigorous economic modernization with stern autocratic techniques designed to ensure his own position at the apex of the Dominican pyramid. A believer in order and progress, Heureaux was the first Dominican leader since independence to direct his energies toward goals other than selling away the national patrimony, enriching himself exclusively, and presiding over national strife.

Under Heureaux, roads were built, railways constructed, irrigation canals dug, and telephone and telegraph lines installed. Immigration increased, and the population grew. The stability that was established encouraged Cuban and other planters to expand sugar production, a step that would have profound implications for the future of the economy. Heureaux kept the Haitians from invading and also survived several challenges to his rule launched from the rich Cibão farm region.

Heureaux was successful in achieving political order and economic modernization, but to accomplish his goals, he was forced to float disadvantageous bank loans and lease the timber-rich Samana Peninsula and its bay (the best natural port in the Caribbean) to foreign interests. Heureaux managed for a time to pay off part of the loans to German, French, British, and U.S. interests, but the debts also demonstrated the degree of dependency of the Dominican economy on foreign capital.

The successes Heureaux achieved in the economic sphere did not lead to a complementary liberalization in the political arena. Instead, as time wore on, he became more autocratic and corrupt. Hired assassins, corrupt sycophants, and networks of spies consisting of the president's mistresses were part of Heureaux's retinue and system of rule. He was a dictator who would court no opposition and did not hesitate to use brutal measures to ensure his unchallenged personal authority.[4]

As Heureaux became more repressive, the opposition mounted. The fact that the president was black further diminished his stature among the white patricians of the Cibão. The Heureaux era came to an end when one of the opposition leaders, Ramón Cáceres, walked up to the president at a crowded public gathering and shot him. The death of Heureaux ended the Dominican Republic's first experiment with a modernizing dictatorship. It would not be the last time a Dominican leader would conclude that national development was only achievable by means of tight control, fear, and a complete dictatorial system.

Heureaux's assassination left another vacuum in Dominican politics that could not be filled by those who had plotted against him. Between 1899 and 1906, the country saw a return of the political factionalism, personal rivalries, and constant infighting that had gone before. The two most prominent leaders were Juan Isidro Jiménez and Horacio Vásquez. Vásquez had been the chief driving force in the anti-Heureaux movement, but he proved a weak and timid leader. Jiménez was a wealthy Cibão landowner who seemed more interested in using the presidency to enrich himself further than in governing effectively.

By 1902, Dominican politics had again become a tinderbox as "Horacista" forces battled "Jimenistas." There were few ideological or programmatic differences between these two factions, but both leaders and their retinues wished to capture the National Palace—and the jobs and treasury that went with it. The conflict between these two factions not only created great instability but also left the economy in shambles. The country's export trade was disrupted, foreign loans were not being paid, and foreign creditors were encouraging their governments to use gunboats to collect unpaid debts.

The near-bankruptcy of the Dominican Republic brought on by political instability and disastrous foreign loans and the threat of foreign powers to use force to collect were the immediate causes of President Theodore Roosevelt's proclamation of his famous corollary to the Monroe Doctrine. U.S. economic and strategic interests in the Dominican Republic had been increasing for some time; the country's present economic difficulties now meshed neatly with the expansionist designs of Roosevelt. At a time when the United States had acquired major interests in the Caribbean (Cuba, Puerto Rico, the Panama Canal) and was determined to play a leadership role throughout the hemisphere, the Dominican Republic's financial problems provided the United States with an opportunity to control the future of its poor, unstable neighbor. Shrewdly sensing how Dominican indebtedness could enhance U.S. influence, Roosevelt negotiated an agreement with interim President Carlos Morales under which 45 percent of the export revenues collected at Dominican customs houses (the principal source of government funds) would be delivered to the Dominican government for current expenses, and the remaining 55 percent would be administered by the United States to pay off the debts.

The receivership agreement between the United States and the Dominican Republic was ratified by both countries in 1907 (the Dominicans had little choice but to go along) and immediately helped extricate the Dominican Republic from its debt of about $295 million. It also increased enormously the U.S. presence (internal revenue agents, administrators, tax experts, *plus* some troops to guard the agents) in the Dominican Republic.[5]

In the meantime, Ramón Cáceres, the assassin of Heureaux, had ascended to the presidency, bringing five years of peace to a country badly in need of tranquility. With the economy and government receipts under the watchful eye of the United States, Cáceres brought political stability, some economic modernization, and much-needed efficient administration. He extended the road system, reformed local government, restructured public enterprises, and brought a level of professionalism to the armed forces. His successes, however, did not fundamentally alter Dominican political habits.

The Jimenista-Horacista conflict continued. Cáceres, while riding in his carriage in Santo Domingo, was assassinated by a Jimenista. The assassin of Heureaux had met his death at the hands of an assassin. Old wounds are not forgotten in the Dominican Republic, and even today, the families involved remain bitter rivals and do not speak to each other. The two dominant figures of turn-of-the-century politics in the Dominican Republic, one an authoritarian modernizer and the other a democratic modernizer, were both slain, victims of the violence, jealousy, and personal rivalries that mark so much of Dominican history.

The death of Cáceres initiated another round of domestic political warfare, economic disruption, and, eventually, foreign occupation. By

1912, the Dominican government was violating the terms of the customs agreement and was slipping again into debt and political chaos. At the same time, the United States shifted its interest in Dominican affairs from economic concerns to political and strategic ones.

By 1916, with the Dominican political situation degenerating, World War I under way, and German influence spreading to Haiti, the Wilson administration began to recognize the need to secure Dominican stability through a military presence. On May 16 of that year, Dominican President Jiménez had been impeached by the Dominican Congress, an action that set off a new wave of rebellion. The reaction of the United States was immediate. The U.S.S. *Dolphin* arrived at the northern coast and began unloading troops. Initially, the U.S. forces did not claim control of the country but sought the more limited goals of restoring order and the 1905 agreement. By November, as it became obvious the Dominicans would not knuckle under to U.S. demands, the U.S. forces already present were authorized to proclaim military rule.[6]

The U.S. occupation lasted eight years. These were years of economic growth, some modernization, and enforced political stability. The U.S. military fostered numerous public works projects (roads, telephones, port facilities), the foreign debt was decreased, educational facilities were built, and public health was improved. It is important to stress, however, that the United States was not so much an "enlightened civilizer" as a "pragmatic occupier." Its "modernization" of the Dominican Republic's land titles system allowed U.S. sugar firms to expand their holdings, the new roads were designed to facilitate the mobility of the occupation military forces, and the public works projects were paid for with Dominican pesos.

The presence of the United States generated considerable opposition. Especially in the east (the sugar areas), bands of patriots (the Americans called them bandits) rose up in armed resistance. The records show the U.S. forces retaliated strongly against the rebels, which may help explain the especially strong anti-Americanism in this area even now. But it must also be said that, unlike Nicaragua, where a guerrilla leader named Augusto Sandino rose to prominence and served as an inspiration for future generations, guerrilla resistance in the Dominican Republic remained limited, and no single charismatic leader emerged. In fact, given the earlier chaos, many Dominicans welcomed the occupation and profited from it.

By 1921, with World War I ended and a new administration in Washington, the United States had lost interest in its Dominican venture. During the next three years, U.S. officials and Dominican leaders worked on a plan that would enable the United States to withdraw militarily while, it was hoped, maintaining political stability and economic solvency.

The agent of stability was to be a new national military force, the *guardia*, trained and equipped by the U.S. Marines. New elections were held in 1924, and aging General Vásquez, leader of the old Horacista faction, was elected president. Two months later, the U.S. flag was replaced by the Dominican tricolor, and that same year, the marines also left.

The U.S. occupation forces left behind them a nation somewhat more prosperous and urbanized than before, a nation that had learned the joys of chewing gum and baseball but had not overcome its past or forgotten old scores, nor was it equipped for democratic government. The marines also left behind a national guard that would henceforth be the final arbiters of Dominican national politics and a young, streetwise lieutenant named Rafael Trujillo, who would use the guard to seize and hold power, rule longer and more brutally than anyone previously in Dominican history, and become Latin America's most totalitarian dictator.

THE TRUJILLO ERA

The six years following the departure of the U.S. forces were stable and peaceful. Vásquez provided a needed respite from the heretofore constant turmoil. The tranquility proved to be only temporary, however, as the nation soon reverted to earlier trends. Rival groups challenged the president and began to plot his overthrow. They accused him of being a puppet of the United States. The president's health failed. The world depression of 1929–1930 ruined the nation's economy. The national guard, left behind by the U.S. Marines and now under the firm control of Trujillo, was a potential destabilizing force. With the country's arsenal in the hands of a highly trained military unit under ambitious leadership, political leaders without a firm base of support would need to be ever vigilant to the threat of a coup.

The fragility of democracy in the Dominican Republic was revealed in 1930 when a revolution was launched from Santiago against the Vásquez government. Rather than defending the government, the clever and ruthless head of the guard instead gave arms to the rebels and assured them he would not block their advance. A one-time telegraph operator and sugar plantation guard, Trujillo had risen rapidly through the ranks of the guardia by faithfully serving the marines. Tough, ambitious, wanting wealth and social position, Trujillo prepared for the day when he could move out of the barracks and into the National Palace.

After Vásquez had been toppled, Trujillo convinced the rebels to lay down their arms. He encouraged the rebel leader, Rafael Estrella Ureña, to run for president. But soon Trujillo was using strong-arm tactics to promote his own candidacy. He now "convinced" Estrella Ureña to run for the vice presidency. Other potential Trujillo opponents disappeared or were found slain, Trujillo's military henchmen used intimidation tactics on the citizenry, and the electoral machinery was taken over by Trujillo. Indeed, he won the 1930 presidential election with more votes than there were eligible voters.

Trujillo's rise to power in 1930 was the result of ad hoc intimidation, manipulation, and fraud. His rule as president and dictator for the next thirty-one years saw the institutionalization of these features and the addition of others; namely, personal aggrandizement, economic control, and brutal and systematic repression. Trujillo would become the most important figure in Dominican history, a leader who presided over a period of tremendous importance in the nation's development and whose mode of operations and policy judgments would touch every aspect of Dominican life. In a real sense, the Dominican Republic became an extension of the dictator, his personal "fiefdom." From 1930 to 1961, he completely dominated the country, holding all power and directly shaping virtually all of its daily activities. Even today, as we have seen, the Trujillo regime remains the most controversial topic in the Dominican Republic, defining its political spectrum, eliciting incredibly conflicting reactions, and largely determining the political views of the population.[7]

Trujillo came to power as a usurper and authoritarian, and the conditions prevailing in 1930 further served the aggrandizement of his power. In September of that year, the most destructive hurricane ever to hit the country leveled Santo Domingo and caused untold damage, injury, and loss of life. Trujillo used the tragedy to consolidate additional authority in his own hands and to rule by decree-law, without constitutional limitations. The depressed economic conditions caused by the market crash of 1929–1930 also enabled him to gather most of the financial reins in his own hands, to move from a system of private capitalism toward one in which the state (Trujillo himself) was the dominant influence, and to subordinate the major economic groups (business, labor, agriculture) to state (his own) direction.

The manner in which he attacked these early problems demonstrated clearly how he would tackle others later. He argued that the country's major difficulties were economic recovery and growth and that it was impossible to talk about freedom and democracy in a country without roads, bridges, docks, agriculture, and so forth. He thus dispensed with all political freedoms.

Trujillo's formula for resolving the nation's economic problems was simple, direct, and not revolutionary. First, he believed, recovery and financial solvency rested on greater economic ties to the United States. To achieve this, he granted the United States vast concessions and power over the Dominican economy—until he later became something of an economic nationalist. Second, he said, economic modernization could not be achieved without major sacrifices from the Dominican people. To that end, he crushed all independent trade unions and squeezed the population dry to acquire capital for development and his own enrichment. Third, those who openly disagreed with his programs were subject to the vast repressive apparatus of the state. With this formula, Trujillo went about the business of moving the Dominican Republic forward while also benefiting himself, his family, and his friends.

In the course of his long administration, Trujillo was responsible for a vast number of building projects and new economic enterprises. This, plus the peace and order of his regime in a country where economic growth and stable politics had been all but completely unknown, accounts for the popularity of his regime—then and now. The Dominican economy, under his strong hand and with favorable sugar prices, expanded at impressive rates.

As the economy flourished, so did Trujillo. Estimates of his wealth ranged from $300 million to about $1 billion. But the monetary figure for his personal wealth may be less important than the extent of his control over the entire national economy. Trujillo or his family members and friends had control of nearly 60 percent of the country's economic assets and about the same percentage of its labor force. They owned the best lands, the majority of the all-important sugar industry, the cement works, airlines, shipping concerns, tobacco fields, and dozens of other enterprises. In addition, most of the gainfully employed population worked for Trujillo, directly in his enterprises or indirectly as government employees.

Trujillo was a realist, which in his time and his part of the world dictated close ties to the United States. He posed as the hemisphere's "foremost anti-Communist" and carefully cultivated favor in the United States. Trujillo tied his administration to the United States with trade, aid, and defense packages that had the important side effect of further bolstering his rule. During the Trujillo years, the Dominican Republic received preferential treatment from the United States. Trujillo made sure the U.S.–Dominican Republic "pipeline" continued flowing by courting the support of presidents and key members of Congress.[8]

What the United States chose to ignore (but which could not be ignored in the Dominican Republic) was the insidious terror and torture Trujillo used to consolidate and maintain his rule. Trujillo turned the Dominican Republic into a vast police state where obedience was a requirement of citizenship and opposition was met with swift and ruthless action.

His terror even reached outside the Dominican Republic, as his agents sought out and executed leading opponents of his rule. Trujillo once went so far as to order the assassination of President Rómulo

Betancourt of Venezuela, but the attempt narrowly failed. For his excesses, Trujillo was condemned both by his own people and by world opinion.

Trujillo ran one of the tightest dictatorships the world had ever seen. The web of controls included military might, political and governmental absolutism, economic monopoly, thought control, educational and intellectual conformity, systematic terror, and control over all socioeconomic groups. But as with any regime that employs such totalitarian excesses, Trujillo and Trujilloism were bound eventually to self-destruct.

In the late 1950s, after thirty years of dominance and seemingly at the height of his power, Trujillo's regime began to break down. Sugar prices, the main source of foreign revenue, plummeted and undermined the economic strength of the country. The assassination attempt against Betancourt resulted in a trade and arms embargo against the Dominican Republic. The United States withdrew its support. Dominican society in the 1950s was also quite different from that of the 1920s. An urban labor force had grown up, and a new middle class had emerged; they were impatient with Trujillo's excesses and monopolistic practices and eager both to liberalize Dominican society and to get a share of the wealth and power for themselves. The domestic opposition grew rapidly.

On May 30, 1961, Trujillo was assassinated along a stretch of highway just west of Santo Domingo while en route to visit his latest mistress. The seven-man assassination team did not represent the most oppressed sector of Dominican society, nor was the assassination accompanied by social revolution. Rather, the group came from the upwardly mobile middle class, from elements once close to the regime who either had personal and family scores to settle or else saw Trujillo as an impediment to their own efforts to gain power and privilege. Though they succeeded in assassinating Trujillo, their plot to seize power failed; all but two of the assassins were subsequently rounded up and killed. The U.S. government was closely involved in the assassination.[9]

The death of Trujillo brought to a close an important chapter in Dominican history and left an indelible mark on the national psyche. As with any political leader who rules for such an extended period of time, Trujillo remains the subject of endless analyses, interpretations, and reinterpretations. Recent examinations of the Trujillo era point to the developmental accomplishments of the dictator, his administrative and organizational talents, and his continuing popularity among many Dominicans who see him as having provided prosperity, normalcy, stability, and a measure of national prestige and power.

But to many others, Trujillo will be remembered as a self-serving and bloody tyrant. His megalomania, torture chambers, corruption, and totalitarianism constitute their lasting picture of Trujillo's regime. Whatever one's final perspective of Trujillo, national savior or national destroyer or some combination of these, the dictator directed the course of Dominican history for over thirty years; the country and its institutions were all tremendously influenced by his rule. With his death, Dominican society experienced a massive collapse of leadership and a political and institutional vacuum. Few Dominicans remembered anything except life under Trujillo. With him gone, the country had to redefine its identity and chart a new course, and it had neither the leadership, the institutions, nor the guideposts to do that.

4

Contemporary Dominican History

Trujillo's death ushered in one of the Dominican Republic's most turbulent eras. No longer was there a single leader who could hold the country together. And because so much power—military, governmental, economic—had been concentrated in Trujillo's hands, the country also lacked a core of middle-level officials who might have stepped into the void. The institutions to preserve continuity were wholly lacking. A variety of elites, old rich and new rich, long deprived of access to power and wealth by the dictator's monopoly, now vied to recapture the National Palace and the funds and positions that went with it. Exile groups returned, and new political parties and labor unions were formed. This was also the time of Fidel Castro's coming to power and of strong efforts by the United States to prevent "another Cuba" in the neighboring Dominican Republic. The Dominican cauldron soon began to boil.

AFTER TRUJILLO

The months immediately after the assassination were chaotic, but the power structure did not change. The news of Trujillo's death did not bring a national outpouring of joy—the Dominican people did not crowd into the streets in victory parades. Instead, the streets remained quiet, filled only with military and secret police units rounding up and sometimes executing—right on the sidewalks—anyone thought to have had a hand in the assassination. The dictator was gone, but the Trujillo system remained intact for the time being.

Power had been inherited by Ramfis Trujillo, the dictator's son, and by Joaquín Balaguer, one of a number of puppet presidents through whom the old tyrant had ruled. They tried to maintain the regime and go about business as usual, but it soon became clear they could not hope to wield the power or exert the authority that Trujillo had for thirty-one years.

39

Domestic opposition mounted. The United States also put pressure on them to democratize. Anxious to push democratic reformism and fearful that another Castro would seize power if it did not, the United States advised Ramfis Trujillo and Balaguer that future good relations between the two countries depended on signs of progress toward democracy.

The Dominican leaders felt the pressure and saw the handwriting on the wall. Within weeks, Balaguer was allowing exiles to return and permitting opposition parties to form. Political activity resumed for the first time in over three decades. Three major groups emerged. The National Civic Union (UCN), which represented the business community and was led by Viriato Fiallo, organized a series of demonstrations and general strikes against the leaders aimed at getting rid of the Trujillo influence. It constituted the strongest early opposition to the regime. Potentially more important than the UCN was the Dominican Revolutionary Party (PRD), a social-democratic party founded in exile by Juan Bosch, who was now allowed to return to lay the groundwork for a popular movement based on social reform. The third group was the Fourteenth of June Movement, whose followers included many students and young people and which came eventually to represent the pro-Castro element.

The pressures from these groups, in concert with Dominican labor and professional associations, further increased the dilemmas for Ramfis Trujillo and Balaguer. They wanted to maintain the Trujillo system and their own positions on the one hand, but on the other, they faced almost daily criticism and pressure from the United States and from their own people, who sensed their weakness.

In November 1961, unable to stem the unrest and not very adept at politics, Ramis Trujillo and the rest of his family fled the country—but not without first emptying the treasury of $90 million. Balaguer remained behind but was forced to share power in a seven-man Council of State that included businessmen, clergy, politicians from the UCN, and the two surviving Trujillo assassins. Inaugurated on January 1, 1962, the Council of State pledged to hold elections before the end of the year.

But stability and democracy were not yet assured. Two weeks after the council's inauguration, a military coup occurred. Two days later, another coup reversed the first one and restored the Council of State but this time without Balaguer, who was forced to leave the country. Balaguer left, however, not as a hated figure like Ramfis Trujillo but with considerable respect. He had helped instigate a cautious democratization, he was not identified with the bloody reprisals of the Trujillos, and he had built a following by vast giveaways of the past dictator's properties. His performance would stand him in good stead later, both among the Dominican people longing for a return to authoritarian normalcy and among U.S. officials looking for a popular but conservative leader.

The second Council of State, now supported by most military units and strongly aided by the United States, sought to preserve order while also providing for gradual democratization. Again made up of conservatives and businessmen and led by lawyer Rafael Bonnelly, the council survived but did not flourish. It was under great pressure to move quickly toward democracy, but because of the social and class makeup of its members, it was often reluctant.

The council achieved some notable successes: It provided freedom and a measure of reconstruction, and it carried out the scheduled elections. But the problems were immense. Most Dominicans knew nothing of democracy or what it meant. Funds were scarce, and the national administration, after so many years under Trujillo, was a shambles. Conservative elites were highly apprehensive about the prospect of democracy, and they proved reluctant to cooperate and ready to find fault. The military, fearing its privileges would be taken away, was restless.[1]

DEMOCRACY AND REVOLUTION

As the parties organized and prepared for December elections, it became increasingly clear that the PRD had the largest popular following. For years, it had been the most active exile opposition group. The party had by now built a strong grass-roots organization in all areas of the country. Its program of social reform under democratic auspices was attractive. And in Juan Bosch, it had an articulate, fiery, charismatic leader.

The election outcome was therefore no surprise. Bosch and the PRD defeated Fiallo and the UCN by a 2–1 margin. The PRD's stunning victory represented the triumph of the urban and rural masses over the country's traditional ruling elites in the upper and upper-middle classes.

The victory also meant an enormous challenge for the new president and his party. Elected on a platform of economic reform and social justice, the new government needed to deliver on its promises to the masses, but at the same time, it had to recognize constraints and deal realistically with powerful conservative and vested interests: the church, the military, the economic plutocracy, and the U.S. embassy.

At first, the Bosch government moved energetically to keep its promise of democratic social revolution. But as the weeks and months passed, it became evident that such extensive changes could not so easily be attained. Some blamed the intransigence of the elite groups, others felt the PRD government was ill equipped to administer the government, and still others saw Juan Bosch as a hapless romantic who could not translate ideology into action. Whatever the reason, the reforms promised by Bosch and the PRD never got off the ground.

Despite the government's lackluster performance, it nevertheless received the concerted opposition of the country's historic ruling groups. The opposition was based more on the potential threat these interests felt than on anything the government actually did. Soon, the church was opposed, the army was rumbling, the economic elites were protesting, and the U.S. embassy became disenchanted. That coalition was enough to topple any Dominican government.

The issue that united them all was anticommunism. Bosch had promised to allow a climate of freedom, including freedom for Marxist groups. That enraged the stand-pat elements, who were convinced the country was about to become another Cuba. They declared the government was infiltrated by Communists. Although the charges were wildly inaccurate and the Dominican Communist groups were woefully weak and disorganized, the truth of the accusations became secondary to the effect they had in unifying the opposition and undermining the government.

The military, led by Col. Elías Wessin y Wessin (soon promoted to general), staged a coup in September 1963, overthrowing the Bosch government after only seven months in office. The coup was bloodless and did not stimulate a widespread progovernment response among earlier supporters.[2]

With Bosch forced into exile in Puerto Rico, the military established a three-man civilian junta soon dominated by Santo Domingo businessman Donald Reid Cabral. But Reid Cabral was not a popular or strong leader. He was viewed as an antidemocratic interloper and as a front for the military. Corruption and repression increased.

The unpopularity and weakness of the government stimulated a renewal of plotting and intrigue—again that familiar pattern. A variety of groups opposed Reid Cabral but often for diverse reasons. Some were interested purely in wealth and personal power. Convinced that the president would never hold the free elections once promised, some PRD activists began a plot to restore Bosch and constitutional government by staging a coup themselves. Leftist students and others planned a Castroite revolution. Businessmen wanted a more honest government that listened closely to them. Rival military factions jockeyed for power, and former president Balaguer was scheming to make a comeback.

On April 24, 1965, the PRD moved to seize power. The revolution was led by both the old PRD civilians and a new group of younger military officers. The rebels struck quickly, taking over key positions in Santo Domingo. PRD leader José Francisco Peña Gómez went on radio to alert the people to the revolution. The announcement sent thousands of people into the streets. Rebel or "constitutionalist" troops occupied the presidential palace. In Puerto Rico, an ecstatic Bosch made plans to return. José

Molina Ureña, formerly head of the Chamber of Deputies under Bosch and thus constitutionally the next in line for the presidency, was sworn in on an interim basis.

But the PRD takeover of the palace and Reid Cabral's fall did not elicit unanimous rejoicing, especially from conservative and military interests or the U.S. embassy. For a short time, the conservatives seemed paralyzed, unable to respond. Meanwhile, as the rebellion spread, Dominicans celebrated Reid Cabral's overthrow and the restoration of constitutionalism.

The celebration was premature. On April 26, encouraged by the United States, General Wessin and the military launched a counterattack. Air force jets strafed the National Palace and rebel strongholds throughout the city. Heavy fighting took place at the Duarte Bridge, the major entry point into the city from the east, where weakly armed civilians repelled the efforts of the military tanks to cross and crush the rebellion.

The early fighting inflicted great loss on the constitutionalists, who could not control the skies and were often cut down by the tanks. They could not convince the military commanders to surrender, nor were they successful in spreading the revolution to the rest of the country. Yet they persevered, and in a decisive battle on April 28, the popular forces drove the military back and seemed on the verge of defeating it.

Although the chief combatants in this civil war were the pro-Bosch constitutionalists against the conservative military, the deciding factor was the United States. Early in the rebellion, the U.S. embassy had made a decision that it did not want Bosch back. Ambassador Tapley Bennett soon began reporting to Washington on the supposed Communist infiltration of the constitutionalist forces. As the conflict went on, it became obvious that the United States was not interested in a cease-fire or a negotiated settlement but favored a victory by loyalist forces to prevent the possibility of "another Cuba."

This initial embassy strategy backfired. Rather than crushing the rebels, the Dominican military disintegrated and seemed poised on the brink of defeat. Rebel military leaders Francisco Caamaño and Manuel Montes Arache took over the constitutionalists' leadership and allied their forces. In some of the fiercest fighting of the war, they pushed the regular military out of the city.

Seeing the military it had counted on to defeat the rebels and restore order about to go under, the United States intervened. On April 28, under President Lyndon Johnson's orders, U.S. military forces were flown into the capital city, ostensibly to protect and evacuate U.S. citizens but in reality to halt the constitutionalist advance.

The buildup of U.S. forces (eventually 23,000 troops) opened a new chapter in the civil war. The U.S. troops surrounded the constitutionalists and ultimately, as in 1916–1924, occupied the entire country. The intervention brought home to Dominicans—and other Latin Americans—the extent to which the United States would go to prevent a possible second Cuba in the Caribbean. The United States was paranoid with this second Cuba complex, intervening in the Dominican case even where no credible Communist threat existed.[3]

It is important to stress at this point that though there were Communist and *Fidelista* elements in the revolution, they were by no means the dominant elements. It was a gross exaggeration on the part of the United States to describe the revolution as Communist inspired or led. The rebellion was an intricate and multifaceted movement made up of several currents. The two most important elements, the PRD civilians and the constitutionalist military, were anything but Communist. Their program was a return to constitutional government not unlike that of the United States.

The realities and complexities of the civil war, however, did not interest Johnson or his advisers. What concerned them was the prevention, at all costs, of a second Cuba. Johnson reasoned that no U.S. president could be reelected if he permitted a second Cuba in the Caribbean; also, in 1965, he was in the midst of preparing for the massive buildup of U.S. forces in Vietnam. His intervention in Santo Domingo was meant to send a message to the North Vietnamese of U.S. strength and a willingness to use it.

Seeking to stabilize the Dominican Republic meant neutralizing the constitutionalists while giving the loyalists a chance to regroup and rearm. To achieve this goal, the U.S. troops established a corridor between the opposing forces. U.S. forces then swept through the city or used the Dominican army to crush the constitutionalists, except in their stronghold in the old city.

Although the U.S. troops stopped short of completely eliminating the constitutionalists, their revolution was aborted. Meanwhile, the United States sought to put a more favorable face on its military intervention by "internationalizing" the peacekeeping forces with small contingents of troops from other countries. The creation of the Inter-American Peace Force (IAPF), hastily assembled under U.S. pressure by the Organization of American States (OAS), did little to alter the realities of the situation. The IAPF was always viewed by Dominicans and other Latin Americans alike as purely a U.S. creation. U.S. military commanders remained in control. Except for the Costa Ricans, all the troops came from countries governed by rightist dictatorships.[4]

The U.S. intervention stimulated intense anti-Americanism. But the United States, once its initial objective of preventing the revolution from succeeding had been achieved, worked tirelessly to extricate itself from the imbroglio. After months of negotiation and on-again, off-again fighting, Colonel Caamaño, the constitutionalist leader, and General Antonio Imbert, who led conservative forces, arranged a cease-fire. The war was brought to a close on August 31, 1965, when both parties, under U.S. pressure, signed an institutional act and an act of reconciliation. The agreements called for the naming of a provisional president and the holding of new elections. Héctor García-Godoy, a moderate Santiago oligarch, became interim president, achieved a modicum of order, and called new elections for June 1, 1966.

Before moving on, it is important to reflect on the 1965 crisis. Much has been written about the revolution and intervention, most of it from a U.S. perspective. Some critics fault the U.S. embassy and its uninformed reporting. Other analysts wonder about the capacity of the United States to deal with profound social and political change in the Third World without falling prey to cold war dogmas and anti-Communist phobias. Still others view the crisis in terms of the larger crisis of the Vietnam War and the emerging role of the United States as policeman of the world. There are even a few individuals who, ignoring all the evidence and accepting the falsifications put out by the U.S. government, actually laud the intervention. Their argument is that the United States stopped the civil war, which eventually enabled stability and democracy to be restored.

Amidst these conflicting interpretations, little attention has been devoted to the meaning of the crisis for the Dominican people and nation. Approximately two thousand Dominicans were killed in the revolution or as a result of the intervention; thousands of others suffered injuries, some permanent. But the social and psychological scars may be just as important. In the revolution, a weak and struggling people and nation had seen their hopes raised, then dashed as the United States intervened. A society that had suffered so much in the past but had persevered and sought a better day was again crushed, spiritually as well as physically.

The revolution of 1965 was not so much about communism as it was about democracy and the Dominicans' ability to manage their own destiny. To the Dominicans, the revolution involved their basic drives as a nation: self-determination, dignity, sovereignty, national pride, that modest place in the sun for which they had always hoped. "In a deeper sense," wrote Piero Gleijeses, "the Dominican crisis began with the arrival of Christopher Columbus at the fair island of Hispaniola." Since the days of Columbus, the Dominicans have had to live not only with underdevelopment but also with the fact of their own weakness and susceptibility to foreign intervention. In 1965, the Dominicans had a chance to overcome their dependency, but instead, they were reminded again of their subservience. It was a hard lesson to master and also one that is indelibly marked on the soul of all Dominicans. They will not forget, but time has by now assuaged the wounds.

THE UNFINISHED REVOLUTION

The Dominican Republic's revolution was an unfinished revolution. The U.S. intervention solved none of the underlying problems—poverty, inequality, and the like—that had caused the revolution; it merely postponed the reckoning. The simmering cauldron that is the Dominican Republic is almost certain to boil over again.

The revolution and intervention had a profound effect on all Dominicans, but it also, we are convinced, had a profound effect on the United States. The United States was caught in a web of lies, its Latin America policy was totally discredited, and the credibility of the government and President Johnson was undermined. The Dominican intervention was probably the first major event leading to the crisis of confidence in the U.S. government that would later reach crescendo proportions over Vietnam and Watergate. One author has written, with a measure of exaggeration but with much truths as well, that the day the United States intervened in the Dominican Republic was the day the United States lost the cold war in the Third World. Hence, the intervention was not only a disaster for the Dominicans; in the long run, it may have been a disaster for the United States as well.[5]

The conclusion of a peace agreement between the contending Dominican factions, the naming of a moderate as provisional president, and the calling of new elections gave the Dominicans a breather, but the scars remained deep. The fighting had brought widespread economic dislocations, intense political antagonisms, and much hatred and bitterness. Although President García-Godoy sought to provide an atmosphere for political and economic reconstruction, there was little possibility of uniting the country for a common development effort. Dominican society was hopelessly divided between the forces of the status quo, who, in most respects, emerged victorious as a result of the U.S. occupation, and the constitutionalists, who saw victory snatched from their grasp and a reimposition of the older system of corruption, authoritarianism, and special favoritism.

Given such divisions, it is not surprising that this era of supposedly "new beginnings" was hopelessly flawed and doomed to failure. The conservative elites now back in power and supported by the United States showed disdain for any opposition to their plan to have the venerable Trujillo puppet, Joaquín Balaguer, brought back and elected president. The opposition PRD and their candidate Bosch, who was allowed to return from exile, were viewed as unacceptable electoral alternatives, especially among the military and police forces.

The United States also supported Balaguer. There had long been an admiration in the U.S. government for this man, who, in contrast to Bosch, was seen as someone who could get things done. The Johnson administration, committed to the social reforms of the Great Society on the domestic front, believed that it could ill afford to gamble on a temperamental democrat like Bosch and felt more comfortable with the conservative Balaguer, even though he signaled a reinstitution of what was now being termed "neo-Trujilloism."

The tactics used to frustrate Bosch's campaign reminded Dominicans that the new ruling groups would not tolerate a fully democratic system. Bosch and his demoralized PRD supporters faced constant threats and recriminations from police and military forces. Some PRD leaders were subject to terrorist attacks that left them wounded or maimed; others were found dead, or they just disappeared. The climate of fear kept Bosch from leaving the capital city, while the systematic repression kept his aides and supporters prudently quiet.

Balaguer, with no fear of reprisals and his campaign lavishly supported by Dominican and foreign funds, moved easily and confidently about the country. He centered his campaign in the campo, where the revolution had not reached, and in the conservative Cibão, where most of the population still lived. Everywhere he went, Balaguer used a low-key approach to instill a sense of confidence and to play down the idea that he was a new Trujillo. To all his audiences, Balaguer pledged to return the country to order, normalcy, and reconstruction. He presented himself as a benevolent father figure, stern but paternalistic.

The result of the 1966 election was as expected. Balaguer won 57 percent of the vote to 39 percent for Bosch. The fact that nearly 40 percent of the electorate literally risked their lives to vote for a man who only campaigned three times out of his house attests to their bravery and to the continued support that Bosch, the PRD, and the liberal democracy commanded in the country. Nevertheless, it is important to stress that Balaguer did win by a landslide. The shy, unobtrusive bachelor had genuine support among certain sectors of Dominican society, including the peasants. Although Bosch and his supporters ignored or chose not to recognize it, Balaguer was not viewed by most Dominican as an ogre or even a *trujillista* but rather as a moderating influence necessary at a time of intense social and political division.[6]

Balaguer's first presidential era, 1966–1978, was one of the most intriguing and, in many respects, one of the most successful in the country's political history. Balaguer defies easy characterization. Some see him as a cunning oppressor of the population, others view him as a tool of U.S. business, still others picture him as a crafty manipulator of the Dominican body politic. Balaguer is all of these—and more. He may best be described as a civilian caudillo. Unlike the gruff, macho, military men who have largely dominated the country since independence, Balaguer is quiet, a poet, ill at ease in front of the cameras and in large groups, not charismatic but hard-working and personally honest. But beneath the quiet demeanor, Balaguer was in complete control of the political system during his first terms, taking instruction from neither his military chiefs nor the United States, confident and aggressive in the right circumstances, a pragmatic reformer, and when necessary, a brutal repressor. Balaguer was both a nationalist and a cautious friend of foreign interests, a pragmatic politician and wily strategist who knew all of Trujillo's tricks and more.[7]

This mixture of outward modesty and inner strength and cunning served Balaguer remarkably well. He largely ignored or silenced his opposition and relegated it to the role of onlooker, while he moved ahead with vigorous economic revitalization. By 1970, Balaguer had consolidated his position and was firmly in command, overseeing an era of unprecedented economic prosperity largely fueled by U.S. assistance and commonly referred to as the "Dominican miracle." With sugar prices skyrocketing, foreign investment flowing in, tourism on the increase, and business, the military, and the middle class all content, the country moved forward with a sense of confidence and drive not seen since the height of the Trujillo era.

Balaguer's accomplishments were many, and he spared no effort in reminding the population of the gains made. These were all presented in highly personalistic terms. It was *his* dam, *his* agrarian reform, *his* housing projects, *his* schools, clinics, irrigation canals, and bridges. Through the constant public relations efforts of his administration, Balaguer was able to present his regime to the world in a favorable light. For domestic and international consumption, the Dominican Republic was pictured as a nation of prosperity, stability, and great progress.

Beneath the hyperbole of Balaguer's public relations effort stood another perception of the Dominican miracle. During Balaguer's first terms, the unemployment rate remained high, at 30–40 percent, illiteracy was in the same vicinity, and most of the population remained locked in poverty and squalor. Although per capita income rose dramatically, this was due chiefly to U.S. pump-priming; the distribution of income remained remarkably inequitable. Most of the new wealth was placed in the hands of the already wealthy and the new middle class; the standard of living of most of the rest of the population actually declined. Malnutrition remained widespread, infant mortality was high, and the social conditions of the poor, especially in the cities, deteriorated. These factors, plus the government's periodic support of right-wing terrorism directed against the PRD, led to another picture of the Dominican Republic—not of progress and democracy, as the government claimed, but of repression and oligopoly designed to serve the needs of the few while the majority went without.[8]

The severe gap between the well-publicized Dominican miracle of Balaguer and the harsh realities of life for the Dominican lower class left the regime with its most serious problem. The government could hold onto power and intimidate the opposition as it did in the 1970 and 1974 elections, but it could never claim that it was popular. With the PRD sitting out the elections, Balaguer won handily, but huge segments of the electorate showed their sentiments by casting blank ballots.

With the Dominican economy supported by revenues from highly volatile sugar prices and sometimes fickle U.S. assistance programs, it was inevitable that the miracle would one day end. By 1970, most of the aid had dried up, and in 1974, oil price hikes by the Organization of Petroleum Exporting Countries (OPEC), a decline in the world sugar market, increased balance-of-payments deficits, high inflation, and even more widespread unemployment threatened the stability of the Balaguer government. Added to the economic woes were numerous charges of military and bureaucratic corruption and heightened disgust with the repressive tactics used by the government.

Balaguer had once been able to revive a flagging government with the announcement of some new grand scheme or massive public works project, but now the aging and ill president began to flounder. Balaguer was no longer seen as an adroit manipulator who could fix everything. The Dominican people were being squeezed more and more—not just the poor, who had always suffered, but now a sizable portion of the middle class, who had once formed the basis of Balaguer's support but increasingly demanded honesty, democracy, and a concern for the legitimate pleas of the lower classes.

With the regime demonstrating weakness, the opposition began to sense an opportunity. The PRD once more revived its rusting grass-roots organization. After being frustrated and intimidated for a decade, the PRD, under the leadership of the moderate millionaire rancher Antonio Guzmán, emerged as the social-democratic alternative to Balaguer.

The 1978 election thus became the first meaningful presidential contest in twelve years. Balaguer was clearly in trouble with the electorate, especially the middle class and the poor, and in Guzmán the PRD had a moderate, effective candidate acceptable to the Dominican oligarchy and the U.S. embassy.

The election provoked a major crisis. Not surprisingly, the military and conservative civilians saw Guzmán and the PRD as a threat to the status quo. Envisioning a shake-up of the high command, fewer opportunities for graft, and possibly an opening up to Havana, the military moved in to seize the ballot boxes and annul the election because the vote count showed Guzmán with an early lead.

Although the action of the armed forces was reminiscent of numerous past interventions in the democratic process, the situation now, in both the Dominican Republic and the United States, had changed. With considerable pressure from the Carter administration and threats of Dominicans to bring the country to a halt with a massive general strike, Balaguer convinced the military to return the seized ballot boxes, and the count was resumed.

After what seemed an inordinately long delay and concessions granted to the *Balagueristas* that included giving them majority control in the Dominican Senate, Guzmán was named the winner with 832,319 votes to 669,112 for Balaguer. World opinion, strong pressure from the Carter administration, and vigilance and direct actions by the Dominicans combined to save the democratic process.[9]

Antonio Guzmán took office in August 1978, to lead the first social-democratic government since Bosch's short and unhappy tenure in 1963. Guzmán promised reform, justice, and freedom and castigated the military for trying to thwart the vote. On hand at the inauguration were some thirty representatives of the United States who reinforced the position of the Carter administration in supporting democracy.

In office, Guzmán moved away from the practices of Balaguer by allowing more political freedom and human rights, challenging the power of the military, stressing more vigorously the obligation of the government in the areas of health care and rural development, and placing tighter controls on foreign investment. It quickly became clear that the Dominican Republic would be run with a greater appreciation of democratic practice and a greater interest in social reform. Yet efforts to change the way government operated and reorder public policy priorities immediately came up against the economic realities of high oil costs and falling sugar prices. The miracle years of the Balaguer era were clearly over as the Dominican Republic faced the prospect of declining export revenues, heightened debt obligations, and growing citizen unrest. Although Guzmán was able to achieve some success in strengthening the democratic climate in the Dominican Republic, he was unable to address the downturn in the economy.

Guzmán struggled with growing criticism from the urban and rural poor who expected more of a social reformer, from the business sector that called for an end to the inflationary cycle and restrictions on imports, and from his own PRD where more leftist leaders such as José Francisco Peña Gómez pressed the president to take a more active role in addressing the needs of the unemployed. What accomplishments Guzmán had made in the areas of professionalizing the military, legalizing opposition parties, and releasing political prisoners were lost amid the clamor for a return to the miracle days of Balaguer.

The disappointing economic performance of the Guzmán administration set the tone for the 1982 presidential election, as Dominican politics became more contentious. The ruling PRD chose as its candidate a moderate lawyer, Salvador Jorge Blanco (Guzmán had pledged not to seek reelection). The nomination of Jorge deeply divided the party because the left wing led by Peña Gómez felt betrayed and began laying the groundwork for a separatist movement. Even more disturbing to those anxious to keep Dominican politics in the center was the presence on the far Left of Juan Bosch and his Dominican Liberation Party (PLD). Bosch had been absent from politics for most of Balaguer's three terms in office, but the failure of Guzmán and the PRD to meet the needs of the masses brought the charismatic leader back into the hunt for the presidency. Despite his absence from politics for several years, Bosch still commanded the respect of many Dominicans and was gaining surprising support from the younger generation. Ever the persistent politician, Joaquín Balaguer also entered the race, promising, as he had in the past, to bring the country back to normalcy.

The power of the PRD's reputation for advocating social change, coupled with the weakness of Bosch's PLD and Balaguer's negative image, allowed Jorge Blanco to win the presidency with 47 percent of the popular vote and a majority in both houses of the legislature. However, his victory was tarnished by the tragic suicide of President Guzmán one month before the inauguration of his successor. The Dominican president, allegedly upset over corruption reports that involved the inner circle of his administration and his family, shot himself in his office. Guzmán's vice president, Jacobo Majluta, took over the reins of power and ushered in a peaceful transition, but the president's death cast a pall over the country as Dominicans worried about the future of democratic government.

The presidency of Jorge Blanco was marked by harsh austerity measures, violent outbursts of urban unrest, widening corruption scandals that reached to the door of the president, a factionalized governing party, and the controversial involvement of the International Monetary Fund (IMF) in the restructuring of the Dominican economy. With sugar prices continuing to drop and export income declining, the Dominican Republic faced a balance-of-trade crisis of enormous proportions. The Jorge government was forced to seek external relief from the IMF, but such relief did not come without concessions. President Jorge was pressured to introduce austerity measures that froze wages, increased prices on staple commodities, cut public sector budgets, and restricted credit. Even though Jorge successfully completed a nearly $600-million loan agreement with the

IMF, his government paid the price in social disorder. In April of 1984, the Dominican Republic was beset by its worst bout of urban unrest since the 1965 revolution. Over one hundred people were killed in a three-day rampage of violence connected to the increase in fuel oil prices.

Although order was restored, the Jorge government lost the support of the people. The PRD president was viewed as bowing to the pressure of the IMF and then using excessive force to put down opposition from those Dominicans who were his natural political allies. The rioting split the PRD further as the moderate wing led by Jacobo Majluta openly feuded with the leftists led by Peña Gómez. Furthermore, the PRD was coming under intense criticism because of recurring allegations that it had used its newly won patronage positions in government to engage in corruption. As the Dominican Republic headed toward the 1986 elections, not only were President Jorge and his policies discredited but the ruling PRD was also viewed as unworthy of public trust and support. From the perspective of the Dominican voter, it was time for a change.[10]

In the Dominican Republic, however, change does not necessarily mean new. As the 1986 presidential election neared, Joaquín Balaguer entered the race, supported by a recently reorganized party. In a savvy political move, Balaguer fused his Reformista Party with the moderate and well-respected Christian Democratic organization to form the Social Christian Reformist Party (PRSC). Despite his age (he was nearing eighty) and failing health (he was legally blind), Balaguer promised the Dominicans that he would bring the country back from the brink. He stressed honesty and hard work, an ambitious public sector works program, and independence from external pressure, whether from the IMF or the United States. Balaguer was not the only candidate seeking to capitalize on the failures of the PRD. A reinvigorated Party of Dominican Liberation (PLD), with a more popular (but also aging) Juan Bosch, was again pledging to speak for the urban and rural poor. No longer a weak organization, the PLD was poised to challenge the established parties with a candidate who spoke the language of the masses. The PRD managed to field former vice president and interim president Jacobo Majluta as its candidate, but the rancor from the nominating convention was so intense that the party was an empty shell.

The election of 1986 was one of the most controversial in the nation's history. With three ex-presidents running for the top government position, the prospect of a close election was real. Furthermore, because of the history of electoral fraud in the Dominican Republic, declaring a winner would not be easy, especially with the voters so divided and tensions running high. As the returns came in, the predictions of a close and contentious election were proven correct. Although Balaguer appeared to have a slim lead, Majluta quickly cast doubt on the results and forced the election into a period of uncertainty that lasted into the summer months. Eventually, after intense negotiations involving the Catholic hierarchy, the Central Election Board, and representatives of the three candidates, Joaquín Balaguer was declared the winner by a margin of 41.5 percent to Majluta's 39.4 percent and Bosch's 18.3 percent. Fortunately, the drawn-out election process did not lead to major outbreaks of violence or military intervention. It appeared that Dominican democracy was strong enough to withstand the conflicts over a controversial electoral process.[11]

Joaquín Balaguer's victory brought back to power one of the great survivors of Dominican politics. Despite his rejection by the people in 1978, Balaguer was able to convince the voters in 1986 that only he could bring the country back from the brink: After all, during his earlier years in power, Balaguer had presided over an economic "miracle." He immediately went to work to revitalize the economy. His major tools were a massive public works program that pumped millions of dollars into public housing projects, roads, hydroelectric plants, and other infrastructure initiatives, along with a willingness to attract foreign investment to the industrial free zones and the agribusiness sector—the same policies that had worked before. Balaguer was keenly aware of the need for regaining the confidence of the business community by keeping inflation low, providing credit opportunities, and widening trade possibilities with the United States and Europe.

But though Balaguer attained a degree of success early in his administration, his spending programs eventually brought on inflation rates in the 40–50 percent range. Budget cutbacks and an unwillingness to address the bloated bureaucracy of public enterprises severely hampered the functioning of basic services such as water, garbage collection, and electricity. Finally, persistent trade imbalances heightened the debt obligations and weakened the standing of the Dominican Republic in international lending circles. By 1988, Balaguer was no longer viewed as the savior of the Dominican economy. Protests over prices, electrical brownouts, wages, and unemployment were seen with disturbing regularity. There was also grumbling that democratic leaders were unable to bring an end to the economic crisis and that the country was nearing collapse. For the first time, Balaguer saw his reputation as an efficient and effective national manager questioned.

With Balaguer no longer able to command public trust, the country headed toward the 1990 elections with growing anxiety. Since the PRD was still enmeshed in factional disputes, the attention turned to Juan Bosch, whose surprise showing of 18 percent in the 1986 election signaled to many that the discontented Dominican electorate might be willing to return the former president to the National Palace. Bosch was encouraged in his campaign efforts by public opinion polls showing him substantially ahead of Balaguer and the PRD. For his part, Balaguer remained aloof from the 1990 campaign, refusing to announce his candidacy even though the whole country assumed that the venerable leader would run again.

To no one's surprise, Joaquín Balaguer ultimately announced his intention to seek the presidency for an unprecedented sixth time. Again, he stressed the familiar themes of managerial capability and hinted at the prospect of a fractured and violent Dominican Republic under the volatile and divisive leadership of Juan Bosch. As the election neared, Bosch played into Balaguer's hand by engaging in an unnecessary attack on the Catholic church. Meanwhile, Balaguer played the elder statesman's role and talked about the future, in particular the part that the Dominican Republic would play in the 1992 celebrations of Columbus's landing in the New World. Balaguer's strategy appeared to be working: Public opinion polls showed the two aging caudillos were running a close campaign and that the margin of victory would be narrow.

The election of 1990 was held under intense international scrutiny as former U.S. President Jimmy Carter led a delegation of observers to the Dominican Republic. As expected, the vote was very close, with Bosch taking an early lead but Balaguer steadily inching closer. There were calls of electoral fraud from the Bosch camp, which claimed that the government-controlled election board was favoring Balaguer. The claims of illegality were dampened, however, by President Carter's statement that the election was "adequate and honest." After a series of recounts, Balaguer was declared the victor by a 20,000-vote margin. Perhaps the most critical electoral fact was that 1.3 million Dominicans abstained from voting as a protest against the failure of democracy to improve the quality of life in their country.[12]

As Balaguer took office in August 1990, he was immediately beset with opposition from PLD stalwarts angry over the election and from a wide range of social groups who demanded action on inflation, debt, unemployment, and the nagging electrical problems. Rather than give Balaguer a honeymoon period, the Dominican quickly began a series of strikes and protests that the government was forced to break up. True to form, Balaguer backed away from some of his more harsh measures and entered into an economic solidarity pact with unions over minimum wages and other working conditions. He also promised to keep prices down and to carefully negotiate with the IMF over a loan agreement that was necessary to restore the Dominican Republic's standing with foreign creditors.

But despite these initiatives and promises, Balaguer could not recover his earlier popularity and was the subject of constant criticism. As a sign of his recognition that he faced popular opposition, in 1991 he announced his intention to call an early presidential election the following year and to change the constitution to forbid two-term presidencies. Political analysts were wary of Balaguer's announcement, suggesting that it was another ploy by the crafty leader to deflect criticism away from his policy failures. Others, however, were more cautious, stating that Balaguer may have recognized that his ability to lead the Dominican Republic had diminished to the point where he would leave politics during the 1992 quincentennial festivities and assume a kind of elder statesman role. Although no one in or out of the Dominican Republic was confident that he or she could predict Balaguer's future, all agreed that the next years would be critical for the country. Not only was the Dominican Republic reaching a historical milestone in 1992, its president was laying the foundation for another round of power politics and political uncertainty.

But the authoritarian strain also remains strong in the Dominican Republic, and it comes increasingly to the surface in times of crisis and economic downturn. Moreover, the long course of Dominican history surveyed here provides few precedents for stable democratic government. What may seem stable and lasting now in the Dominican Republic can, as stated in the provocative title of a book about the country by former ambassador John Bartlow Martin, be quickly "overtaken by events."

5

Social Structure and Social Groups

The historical legacy of the Dominican Republic is a mix of retarded political development, centralized control by dominant leaders, and brief periods of economic prosperity and governmental stability. But what of the more fundamental social, economic, and political conditions that underlie this history and have produced such a mixed legacy? The repeated incidents of domestic strife, foreign intervention, national and international breakdown, despotism, and dependency that figure so prominently in Dominican history are in fact manifestations of more basic socioeconomic and sociopolitical problems that emanate from the very foundations of national life.

SOCIAL STRUCTURE

No single factor is sufficient to explain the persistence of the Dominican Republic's underdevelopment and its problems as a nation. But surely the prevailing class and social structure must be placed at or near the top of the list. The historical social and racial separation of the classes, the rigidities of the social structure, the two-class system, the emergence now of a middle class, and the growing polarization and potential for class warfare are all essential factors in enabling us to understand the Dominican system—and the recent changes occurring therein.

Any discussion of the Dominican social structure is best begun by stating that the Dominican Republic is a deeply divided and unequal society. Vast gaps separate the classes, and the stark realities of class separation can be found everywhere—in clothes, housing, language, opportunities, jobs. As with many racially complex societies, these differences are both socioeconomic and racial.[1]

Race and class are closely interrelated. Those at the top of the Dominican social pyramid tend to be white, of European background.

57

Those at the bottom are not only poor, they tend also to be black, descendants of the original slaves or more recent arrivals from Haiti brought in to cut sugarcane. In between (and numerically the largest group) is the mulatto population. Much of the new middle class comes from the mulatto element, though within this group there are both further sharp economic gradations and various racial subtypes.

The white elite has historically dominated the nation's social, political, and economic life. But there are avenues for ambitious poorer (and darker) individuals to rise in the social scale, chiefly through politics and the army. Those who attend diplomatic receptions in Santo Domingo will probably note that the civilian, banking, and (old) moneyed interests there will be white or light mulatto and will congregate on one side, while the military officers, generally darker, will congregate separately. But the military is also a route to wealth and power, and the Dominican Republic has thus had more black and mulatto presidents than any nation in the western Hispanic world. Yet this is a statistic about which the Dominicans have very ambiguous feelings—a measure of their preoccupation with race.

From a cold statistical viewpoint, the class differences in the Dominican Republic are stark. The bottom 50 percent of income earners receive 18.5 percent of the national income, while the top 10 percent receive 38.5 percent of the national income. Although there were periods in the 1970s when the gross domestic product (GDP) increased by rates in excess of 5 percent and per capita income rose dramatically, the 1980s and 1990s have been periods of low or even negative GDP rates, and the per capita income has stagnated near the $1,000 level, thus keeping the nation poor and preventing it from breaking out of its Third World status. Moreover, what new wealth has been generated in the Dominican Republic has, in large part, benefited the business and professional class, while the urban and rural masses have seen little change in their incomes or their lives.

With a minimum wage of $111 a month in the private sector and $80 in the public sector (and far less when wage laws are enforced), with pay in the agricultural sector averaging $3.50 per day (paid only on the days worked), and with an unemployment rate of about 30 percent (plus another 20 percent underemployed), it is clear that poverty is the situation of life for most of the Dominican population. Life for them is a real and constant struggle to provide the basic necessities of food, shelter, and clothing. Poverty is visible in the bloated bellies of many of the children, in the inadequate housing and health facilities, and in the diseased and malformed bodies of many adults.

Although the 1980s and 1990s have not seen an improvement in the living standards of the poor (infant mortality, for example, has more than doubled since 1978, and life expectance and literacy rates have seen only minor improvements), the situation of the Dominican middle and upper classes reveals a much different situation. They have done quite well even in the midst of an economic downturn. However, there are now several elites in the Dominican Republic: an older gentry class, a business-commercial elite that emerged around the turn of the century, a new rich class associated with Trujillo, and an even newer rich elite whose wealth is in land, banking, the professions, light industry, and tourism. All these elites profited enormously from the Balaguer era.

The upper classes worry about different things than those at the pyramid's bottom. Whereas the latter must concern themselves with basics such as jobs, food, housing, and survival, the former focus on such issues as the world market price for sugar (critical to the country's wealth and their own), the waxing and waning of U.S. power and investments (also crucial to this group's position), trade patterns, the future of tourism, family ties, and gossip. The perspectives of the upper classes are concentrated outwardly on their relations with their large North American neighbor and internally on the need for order, discipline, and building a national infrastructure. Little talk about poverty or unemployment emanates from their plush homes in the western sectors of Santo Domingo, their farms in the Cibão, and their vacation houses in the mountains.

The gap between rich and poor in the Dominican Republic thus involves more than money or economic statistics. It is an attitudinal gap between persons inhabiting entirely different worlds. For one group, the concerns are immediate, basic, and tied to life-sustaining activities. For the other, the concerns are wider and longer-range, involving broader worlds. These two groups are far apart; they touch occasionally (the wealthy have maids and get their shoes shined), but they do not meet. These gaps not only imply a vast separation between the social classes but also mean, perhaps inevitably, the potential for class conflict. With little in common and so much distance between them, the upper and lower classes both sense that one day there will be war between them— that and other uncomfortable facts of life are usually covered over with characteristic Dominican politeness.

URBAN AND RURAL POVERTY

The sheer poverty of most of the population (perhaps 80 percent) is, to the visitor, the single most striking and immediate feature of the Dominican Republic. The tourist brochures that present the country as a romantic vacation playground or a step backward in time to the swash-buckling days of Columbus say nothing of the tin and wood shanties along Santo Domingo's Ozama River or the numerous poor neighborhoods that surround the city. In fact, along the beautiful stretch of the Caribbean that leads from the airport to the tourist hotels, the Dominicans have done a good job of hiding their poverty. It is something to be ashamed of, to disguise so that foreigners will have a good impression.

Nonetheless, the poverty is stark, real and plainly visible to all who care to see. In the poor neighborhoods, there are open sewers, naked children with bloated bellies, unemployed young men, and always, faces with the forlorn gaze of poverty and malnutrition. To the poor urban dwellers, a normal day includes the usually fruitless search for employment, endless hanging around, a continuous struggle to manage an insecure household in the face of accelerating price increases for such staples as rice and beans, constant shortages of basic foodstuffs, and a climate of despair and rising violence.

It is in the cities where the poverty seems most stark, particularly when seen against the most visible signs of modernity: new skyscrapers, vast building projects, ostentatiously displayed wealth. Such contrasts serve as a reminder of how much needs to be done in the Dominican Republic, and they indicate how unevenly modernity has come. The recent thrusts toward development and economic growth have largely passed by the urban poor, turning them into a vast army of disadvantaged who may pose a major threat to the elite-dominated social and political structure. But these poor Dominicans are no longer passive; they have demonstrated and struggled for decent housing, a modicum of public services (water, electricity), and, most importantly, jobs. It is these barrio residents who took to the streets in the bloody riots of 1984 and who have kept the pressure on the Balaguer government ever since with regular street demonstrations, strikes, and violence. Increasingly, these poor urban residents are forming neighborhood organizations to demand jobs, better daily wages, and the full range of government services, from housing to trash collection.

The anomaly of the Dominican urban poor is that despite their political influence through the PRD and now the PLD, their great numbers, and their vast anger against the status quo, little change has come to the barrio. Despite the industrialization and economic stimulation of the Balaguer era, things remain the same for the poor—the housing situation and services have actually gotten worse. With reformist PRD governments in 1978 and 1982 and pledges by Balaguer in 1986 and 1990 to turn the economy around, the urban poor have waited for political leaders to deliver on their many promises. But the nation's economic and social problems are so enormous and the means of resolving them so limited that hope is wearing thin, cynicism abounds, and the potential for renewed violence is rising. Genuine class conflict has also increased.

The poverty of the urban centers is starkly visible, creating severe tensions and periodic outbreaks of violence, but rural peasants endure their poverty in a different setting and reveal their frustrations in a less overt manner. Rural poverty is less visible because the contrasts are not so great; it is also a poverty that is "quiet."[2]

Campesinos live a simple life of hard work, few pleasures, and little hope of improvement. If they are lucky enough to own a small parcel of land (300,000 families own tracts of less than 5 acres), it is probably poor rocky land that barely yields a subsistence, is inadequate for a family, and gives insufficient surpluses to sell in the market. The chances are even greater that the campesino has no land at all, however, working occasionally as a tenant farmer or sugarcane harvester. The work is long and arduous, the pay extremely low, and protection against disability, old age, or unemployment nonexistent.

The Dominican Republic's statistics on illiteracy, unemployment, life expectancy, and per capita income are dismally low when presented as *national* figures, but the situation in the countryside is actually far below the national average. Unemployment in the campo may be as high as 50 percent, illiteracy 80 percent, life expectancy at least ten years below the national figure, and incomes far below those in the urban areas.

The terrible poverty of the rural population has not yet led to the violence and class conflict that now seems endemic in the cities. There is an attitude of resignation to one's fate in the campo. The traditional paternalistic ties between landlord and peasant remain strong and greatly influence the character of politics. The peasant remains generally conservative, as yet unattracted to appeals for guerrilla revolution. For example, in the 1965 revolution, the fighting was largely confined to the capital, while the countryside remained marginal to the conflict. In this regard, the urban and rural poor exhibit little solidarity in a class sense.

There are encouraging programs to bring social justice and new possibilities to the poor, and the situation in the Dominican Republic is not entirely without hope. Balaguer's public works projects, particularly in the area of housing, have addressed one of the major sources of distress for the poor. The placement of industrial free zones throughout the countryside in small and medium-sized cities has also helped to ease the transition from a largely agricultural economy to a more diversified one. Furthermore, the increase in foreign investment in agribusiness enterprises has begun to fill the void left from the downturn in sugar,

Despite these positive developments, the path to change for the poor in both urban and rural areas is long and strewn with countless roadblocks. The push toward industrialization with the free zones and the expansion of the tourist sector have not kept pace with population increases and the yearly demand of young Dominicans seeking employment. And in spite of the highly touted free zones, the 120,000 jobs generated by the assembly plants have not been the answer to the 30 percent unemployment rate in the Dominican Republic. As critics are quick to point out, many of the assembly plants are capital- rather than labor-intensive concerns, creating an efficient operation but not necessarily generating employment. Moreover, there are increased incidents of labor trouble in the zones as workers complain about union busting and poor working conditions. As a result, Dominicans are "protesting with their feet" as they leave the country for Puerto Rico or the United States. Those that stay behind to compete for jobs find that the prospects for successful employment often depend on the investment or vacation decisions of foreigners.

There are those who also fault the weak and divided union movement in the Dominican Republic, alleging that it contributes to limiting opportunities for the urban and rural poor (only 12 percent of the workers are organized in eight separate and competing confederations). Tied closely to political parties, unions have been more successful at gaining access, favors, and patronage than at winning significant economic rewards for their members. There have been some signs recently that the unions are more willing to join forces and demand higher wages from government, but in a country with limited budget resources, an unlimited supply of cheap unskilled labor, and a desire to attract foreign investors to a probusiness climate, there is little interest in promoting legislation to reform wage rates and working conditions. In the past, especially under the Balaguer government, increases in the minimum wage were denied until tensions rose to the point that they had to be defused with concessions. Both the unions and the government then joined in an agreement that temporarily stopped the crisis.

In the rural areas, different roadblocks stand in the way of change. At the heart of the problem is the lack of sufficient arable land. Only about 50 percent of the total territory is arable. What arable land is available is not always used effectively. Many wealthy landowners, for example, prefer to keep their rich lands as pasture and not under cultivation because cattle and vast acreage are symbols of lordly status. Less than half of the rich Cibão Valley is under cultivation.

The intransigence of the landed elites lies at the core of the country's frustrated efforts at agrarian reform. This, in turn, is reinforced by a centuries-long tradition that affords social standing on the basis of the ownership of land. Land is viewed as both an economic investment and a source of social and political power. The lands inherited from Trujillo and once intended for agrarian reform, for instance, have since been swallowed up by ambitious government and military officials, who see the ownership of land as the symbol by which they will gain upper-class status. Generations of landlords are not easily convinced that their status must be sacrificed to defuse social tensions or attain a newly defined standard of social justice.

So far, attempts by the government to change the land system have not been successful. Bosch was overthrown in 1963 in part because of his land reform proposals. On numerous occasions, angry landowners protested Balaguer's plans to limit the size of landholdings. The government's agrarian reform efforts have been quite limited, with the president more interested in handing out provisional land titles in a piecemeal fashion (as is typical of his paternalistic style) than in engaging in a large-scale distribution and equalization program. Although the Balaguer government's agrarian reform efforts were quite limited, the strong reaction of owners even to the proposals of a conservative government indicates how sensitive the issue is. Balaguer settled for a much reduced program that gave provisional titles to peasants for unused government land of low quality.

The efforts to effect social change and alleviate the problems of poverty and inequality are thus mired in complex, long-term social and power relationships, in the necessities of modern industrial development that call for a postponement of expensive social programs, and in decades, even centuries, of poverty and neglect. The Dominican lower classes remain trapped in poverty with few possibilities for improvement. Government development strategies that seek to pull society forward by means of industrialization and the modernization of infrastructure may be sound policy at one level, but they have had little effect or even a deleterious impact on the 80 percent who remain untouched by the economic opportunities that have been afforded the business and professional class.

THE EMERGING MIDDLE CLASS: AGENT OF CHANGE?

The inequality existent between the 5 percent of the population who enjoy wealth, status, and power and the 80 percent who live in abject poverty is perhaps the most important and obvious feature of the Dominican social structure. But sandwiched between these two groups is a rising middle class, about 15 to 20 percent of the population, whose political influence is now commensurate with its rising economic power.

The role of the middle class in Latin America, however, remains controversial. Is it a force for reaction or a force for democracy? The answer is, it depends. The middle class generally favors modernization, development, and democracy at a stage when it is trying to wrest control from the old oligarchies and needs support in its quest from urban workers. Once it has achieved power, however, the middle class has tended to turn conservative, employing the military to keep the lower classes in place.

In the Dominican Republic, the middle class is small, but its importance is out of proportion to its size. Its ranks include government workers, army officers, small-business people, students, teachers, clerics, doctors,

Artist with his sculpture (*Warren Smith; courtesy of Public Affairs Analysts, Inc.*)

lawyers, technicians, and professionals of all sorts. These are all "influentials," the opinion leaders. The middle sectors are dominant in some of the most important national institutions: officer corps, church, bureaucracy, universities, political parties, and trade union leadership. Some would say the middle class has become the most important social group in the country.

The era of the so-called Dominican miracle under Balaguer in the 1970s helped expand the middle class's ranks and popularize its way of life. Those who traveled to Santo Domingo during the days of the revolution or in the postrevolution period will hardly recognize the city today. New middle-class neighborhoods have sprouted all around; the focus of business, commercial, social, even governmental affairs has shifted from the old center to the suburbs; and a great variety of movie houses, car dealerships, supermarkets, discotheques, and other amenities of middle-class existence have blossomed.

The middle class is diverse politically. Some of its members are cautious about politics, some are apathetic. Many are conservative, forming the opposition of Bosch in the early 1960s, the loyalist camp in the 1965 revolution, and the early basis of support for the Balaguer government. But many others hold more liberal and democratic values. It was also the middle class that supported Juan Bosch and his constitutionalists in 1965. And when Balaguer's government in the 1970s become too repressive and corrupt, the middle class abandoned it and went over to the opposition. In 1978, when the military sought to frustrate the popular vote for Antonio Guzmán, it was middle-class businesspeople, shopowners, doctors, and lawyers who protested the most ardently. But when the PRD presidents failed to restart the miracle and used government for their personal gain, the middle class was the first to grumble about the deteriorating economic climate and call for the return of Balaguer; this group also stayed with Balaguer in his 1990 campaign against Bosch, thus completing a full circle of support and abandonment.

The contradictions within the middle class are best explained by the diverse groups making up that sector. The upper middle class, consisting of important businesspeople and well-established professionals, tends to be most conservative, aspiring to or holding elitist values that the elites themselves no longer hold. High-ranking military officers (colonels and generals) also fall within this group. The middle middle class, consisting of government planners and economists, teachers and university students, younger professionals and military officers, represents a more mixed group; they often favor reform and support the PRD, but some of their members are quite conservative. The lower middle class is a swing group: Its economic and social position is precarious, leading it to support stable and conservative causes, yet when corruption becomes so widespread that its normal activities suffer, this group can also swing to support reformist movements.

The great diversity of the middle class makes generalizations about its political behavior difficult. What can be said safely is that the middle class is growing and will exercise an increasingly important role in the national life. This is a relatively new development, begun under Trujillo when a sizable middle class began to grow and accelerated during the prosperity and stability of the Balaguer years.

Not only is the middle class larger, but it also has definite viewpoints on many political matters, and its members have the controlling voice in most of the nation's institutions. However, the middle class still speaks with many voices, ranging from the far Left to the far Right. It is so deeply divided that one cannot speak of a middle-class society—stable, moderate, middle-of-the-road—emerging as yet in the Dominican Republic. Thus, whether this middle class will evolve as a stabilizing influence, as U.S. officials fervently hope, or will continue as a divided *and* divisive element cannot be clearly ascertained at this stage.

CLASS AND CLASS CONFLICT

The Dominican Republic is a nation deeply fragmented along class and racial lines. Because the 1965 revolution was both a political and a class revolt that was frustrated and remains unfinished, many observers have predicted an imminent renewal of the struggle. Yet the defeat of the constitutionalists and the restoration of elite and bourgeois rule under Balaguer did not usher in a period of renewed conflict. There have been occasional flare-ups against price increases, police brutality, and fraudulent electoral practices, but the disturbances have been isolated and have not involved any sustained class challenges to the system. Why?

The relative absence of social and class conflict in the Dominican Republic until recently can be analyzed from a variety of perspectives. One view commonly expressed by moderates and conservatives is that life for the general population has not been all that bad. The country, it is said, has returned to a climate of normalcy where social and political antagonists have been put aside in favor of a concerted effort to achieve economic development. The proponents of the normalcy position see the 1965 uprising as an aberration instigated by a small group of malcontents. They say the historical legacy, cultural foundations, and psychological makeup of the Dominicans are not conducive to large-scale social unrest. The paternalistic and patron-client-centered concept of politics and the deep-seated respect for traditional social relationships militate against class conflict. The normalcy reigning since 1965 is then a reflection of the *real* Dominican Republic. This argument asserts that the spirit of politeness, gentleness, cooperation, respect for authority, and resigned acceptance of adversity serve as safeguards against destructive class warfare.

There is considerable truth in these arguments, but it is by no means the whole truth. Dominicans *are* conditioned by their historical and cultural tradition, and they are, like the rest of us, creatures of habit. But they are also very pragmatic. Lacking arms and an organizational base, it is quite prudent for the Dominican lower classes to remain quiescent for now. Martyrdom for some presumably glorious cause may be attractive to the young but not to those who are older or have a families to provide for. To them, it makes no sense to get killed if there is no chance of success; a better strategy is patience, forbearance, waiting for an opportunity (as in 1965) when the possibility of winning is greater.

For example, after he and the PLD lost the presidential election to Balaguer, Bosch went before the voters in 1990 and asked for massive demonstrations, strikes, and public support for a rejection of the results. Although there was some response to Bosch's call, no massive outcry by the people occurred. Later, however, when Balaguer took office, opposition to his lack of initiative on economic reforms turned violent as numerous incidents of urban and rural unrest were staged throughout the country in 1990 and 1991. But here as well, Balaguer often quieted the demonstrations by agreeing to short-term solutions or compacts between the government and labor representatives that provided some price and wage guarantees. This piecemeal approach weakened the opposition and returned the country to a temporary normalcy with little but cosmetic changes.

Another very concrete reason for the general social calm since 1965 has to do with the weakness of the leftist groups in the Dominican Republic and government repression of them. Since 1961, when the political system was opened up, the Left and Marxist groups have enjoyed little popular support. One can find Marxist groups in the country, but their political influence has been small. Poorly led and lacking organization, they have not had the strength to challenge, let alone take over, a government. After the revolution, when leftist groups like the Fourteenth of June Movement, the Dominican Popular Movement (MPD), and the Communist Party either disbanded, went into exile, or were suppressed, there were few who lamented their eclipse. And when some of these same groups sought to foment guerrilla warfare in the Dominican countryside, they were unable to mobilize popular support and were eventually snuffed out by the military. Popular disinterest and government repression have kept the far Left weak and divided.

The Dominicans have not generally explained their plight in Marxist terms. Today, if there is any fervent ideological sentiment among the people, it is generally expressed in terms of a quest for liberal democracy.

The conflicts in the Dominican Republic have not been aimed at achieving democratic and constitutional government, respect for basic human rights, and more traditional liberal precepts. Added to this growing interest in and respect for democracy is an interest in the market economy and the operation of private sector development. Like many of their Latin American neighbors, large numbers of Dominicans are quickly embracing capitalist principles and touting the wonders of free trade, economic restructuring, and privatization.

Still another reason for the absence of manifest class conflict in the Dominican Republic is the continuing influence of personalistic politics. The history of the Dominican Republic has been one of the conflict more between strong leaders than between rival ideologies. This is changing, but leadership—or the perceived absence thereof—is still crucial for explaining the ups and downs of national politics. Strong leaders provide continuity, unity, and stability—for a time; weak leaders invite movements directed against them. The 1965 revolution was not just an ideological and class conflict; it was also an effort to restore coherence and leadership and to replace the floundering and ineffective Donald Reid Cabral.

The "leadership principle" also helps to explain the large following of president Joaquín Balaguer. Despite his isolation from the people, his centralized style of management, and his inability since 1986 to return the Dominican Republic to the miracle days, Balaguer has remained a respected (but not popular) figure, even to some sectors of the lower class. He has had an uncanny ability to avoid ideology and personal or class attacks, and he stresses his personal competency and honesty. This ability to highlight his talents for leadership and management has unfortunately begun to break down. His deteriorating eyesight, the failure of his economic recovery programs, and the persistent collapse of public services have called into question his ability to rely on his personal reputation or on patronage to assuage class unrest. Balaguer's style of making personalist appeals for patience and working out last-minute compromises is not working so well anymore. What worked in the 1970s and even in the 1980s may not be enough to control the anger of people in the 1990s who want more out of their leaders than patchwork solutions and incremental changes.

Although the grounds for class conflict and social unrest are present in the Dominican Republic, there are other factors tending to militate against a violent upheaval. The catalyst that might set off the conflagration is often hard to pinpoint; the Dominicans are not easily aroused to violent tactics. They have, historically, been a conservative people influenced strongly by traditional social relationships, beliefs, and forms of leadership.

It would be a grave miscalculation, however, to conclude that the chances of future violence and upheaval are minimal. The frustrations that breed on poverty, inequality, and injustice are many and profound. Although presently latent, violence could explode again as it did in 1965, 1984, and again in the 1990s. If and when such violence comes, it will likely be resorted to with great reluctance, probably as a result of pent-up anger over economic policies or shortages of basic commodities. Although it is always possible that violence will be politically focused, as it was in 1965, the Dominican Republic of the 1990s is a country where disputes are generated mainly by economic conditions and economic decisions and less so by who is in power. If widespread and intense class conflict does come, it will be because the government has tinkered with public policies without engaging in a massive overhaul of a system that has bred inequality and injustice. But surely one of the lessons of the 1965 revolution is that when provoked, the Dominican people will fight to the death.

GROUP DYNAMICS AND THE DOMINICAN SOCIAL SYSTEM

Dominican society is sharply divided horizontally in terms of the several classes present. For this reason, it is absolutely necessary that one employ class analysis to help explain the nation's politics and political economy. But Dominican society is also structured vertically, in terms of occupational, functional, and power groups. Both perspectives are necessary in order to understand the workings of the system.

Dominican politics is often dominated by the interplay of key power contenders and corporate groups. These include family and kinship groups, the army, the church, the economic elites, students, labor, and the Americans. These groups form a patchwork of contending factions and interest groups acting and interacting on the basis of self-interest, moral or ideological principle, or simply raw power. We shall be looking at each of these major groups in turn.

Family and Kinship Groups

Family and kinship (extended family) groups are still every important in the Dominican Republic. Who is related to whom, who is the godfather of whom, who owes whom what kinds of favors–these are all vital questions to the Dominicans; these questions are also critical in shaping the national political system. Clean versus dirty business deals, social and family slights, what one person's grandfather did to another person's grandfather—these can be issues of major national importance. Particularly in a country where everyone who counts knows everyone else or is interrelated, such personal and family relations take on major significance.

What is often covered over with the language of partisan or ideological conflict may be more basically the expression of such conflicts between rival families. Political parties, at least the traditional ones, are often just family cliques devoid of genuine program or ideological differences. Similarly, the complex interrelations between civilian and military elites are often governed more by family ties or patronage connections than by policy differences.

Foreigners on brief visits to the Dominican Republic often have a hard time sorting out what goes on in front of the Dominican curtain and what goes on behind it. The former is visible, public, for the world to see; the latter is private, hidden, secretive. Those who stay there longer come to realize that behind the partisan and ideological conflicts that are public is a web of family and personal relations that are private. To really understand Dominican politics, one must come to grips with these family, kinship, and interpersonal relations, as well as with the more manifest and visible interest-group dynamics.

The Military

Among organized groups, there is no question that the military holds the balance of power in the country. Recalling Dominican history should be sufficient to indicate how often power has rested in the hands of the generals.[3]

At first glance, the military would not appear to be such an imposing force. It numbers 33,000 men: 14,000 in the army, 4,500 in the navy, 4,500 in the air force, and 10,000 in the national police. Its budget is about 10 percent of total public expenditures. The Dominican armed forces are much smaller and less well equipped than neighboring Cuba's, and their share of the budget is considerably less than it was in Trujillo's time and in the 1960s. In fact, the Dominican military in recent years has complained that its equipment is out of date and insufficient to meet the security needs of the nation, particularly in the area of drug interdiction. The Dominican government has been working with the United States to modernize the armed forces, not only because of the drug threat but also because the country still is viewed as a strategic U.S. ally, with Communist Cuba nearby and volatile Haiti next door.

The manpower and budget figures, however, do not reflect the military's power. Its purpose is not so much to defend the nation's frontier and beaches from foreign aggressors as to serve as an internal occupation force and political instrument. Although the Dominican Republic has been governed almost continuously by civilian leaders since Trujillo's death in

1961, every government has been on probation to the military and must recognize realistically the military's capacity to seize power. The military is always in the background, not necessarily seeking power but adamant that power be wielded in a manner that does not threaten its prerogatives or destabilize the fragile sociopolitical order.

The military's strength and influence force presidents to play a dangerous game of political manipulation. Modern presidents from Balaguer to Guzmán have seen fit to shuffle military officers in and out of command or governmental posts in order to weaken their ability to plot against the administration. Payoffs and cushy opportunities for enrichment have also been given officers, especially in the area of trafficking in illegal drugs, where the military is constantly the brunt of rumors.

Antonio Guzmán began the move to weaken the military's power. After assuming office, he retired 23 senior officers and 243 noncommissioned officers in an attempt to get rid of the potentially disloyal pro-Balaguer groups. The key man that he replaced was Gen. Enrique Pérez y Pérez, a Balaguer loyalist who had also been linked to the death squads operating in the early 1970s. Pérez was offered the ambassadorship to Spain and an attaché's position in London. After rejecting both, Pérez retired with a hefty pension; he made a commitment that he would stay out of politics. Joaquín Balaguer built on Guzmán's efforts to loosen the military's hold on politics and added his own unique strategies. He in particular has developed a reputation for being the master of moving military officers in and out of positions of power and prestige as a means of keeping the armed forces off guard and, more importantly, ensuring his own political survival. On a number of occasions, Balaguer did not hesitate to remove the heads of all the armed forces and replace them with new (and perhaps more loyal) officers.

But efforts to depoliticize the military can never be complete. The armed forces are a political agency, and their officers are divided into groups with partisan objectives. Moreover, what Balaguer has learned over the years—and what future presidents should recognize—is that keeping the military at bay and supportive of civilian rule often requires looking the other way and providing the armed forces with the budgets and pay increases that will maintain their support. For all its public declarations, the military ultimately backs democratic rule because the officers hold influential positions in governing circles and have numerous opportunities to advance their personal interests. Should a president take action to weaken that influence and threaten those interests, the military's pledge to support democracy will certainly come under review. A prudent president must walk a tightrope between these contending factions. Rumors of coups and coup preparations occur frequently. In 1979, Guzmán nipped in the bud a coup attempt by a group of disgruntled officers, but the incident served as a reminder of the tenuousness of the civilian government's position.

The Church

The Dominican Catholic church is not as strong a force as it once was. Understaffed, not wealthy, with few programs, the church cannot exert strong pressure. Despite the fact that the Dominican Republic is a Catholic country and its education, social, and political institutions are infused by precepts of Catholic culture, the church as a political agency is not very powerful. (During recent presidential elections, however, it was the church hierarchy that played the role of mediator between rival political factions and eventually crafted the settlement that brought an end to the disputes that were threatening stability and democracy.)

The church served for a long time as a prop of the Trujillo regime, and in earlier days, its voice in telling parishioners how to vote was influential. It was identified with reactionary and conservative causes. But the church has modernized itself and can no longer be identified automatically with the status quo. It does not have the personnel or the resources to be more than a secondary voice in national politics, and as the Dominican Republic has become more secular and middle class, the church's influence has diminished further. It is still influential on some issues—divorce, population control—but it is significant that the Dominican Republic has both an official family-planning program and legislation that has made the country a haven for "quickie" divorces.

The voice of the church is still important, but it is no longer part of the old triumvirate of power (church, army, oligarchy), and in comparison with other groups, its influence is no longer decisive. Further, the presence of Protestant missionary groups and small fundamentalist churches in the Dominican Republic has become an issue of continuing concern, especially as more Dominicans become attracted to the simple messages of hope and redemption offered by the new religions.

Economic Elites

Although the church's influence has diminished over time, that of the economic elites has increased. Particularly as the nation has modernized, become more affluent, and involved itself more in international markets, the power of business groups has correspondingly increased.

The Dominican Republic is no longer governed by a small landed oligarchy. Rather, the landed oligarchy has also gone into business, and meanwhile, a whole new class of bankers, industrialists, financiers, factory owners, managers, owners of commercial establishments, and importers-exporters has appeared. In 1963, the business groups were influential in overthrowing Bosch's democratic government, but today, their numbers and influence are even greater than they were then.

The economic elites are organized into a chamber of commerce and associations of industry, commerce, and landowners. They are wealthy, often well educated, and always well connected. Especially under Balaguer, they have direct pipelines into the government and have received the advantage of knowledge of pending government economic decisions. Their influence is great not just because they are well connected but also because the whole nation is dependent on them for jobs, financial expertise, and continuing prosperity. It is said in the Dominican Republic that the military is the ultimate arbiter of national politics but that the economic elites run the country on an everyday basis.

Students

University students must sometimes by reckoned with in Dominican politics, but their power is not nearly as great as that of the armed forces or the economic elites.

There are now 90,000 students enrolled in six universities. The center of student activity is the Autonomous University of Santo Domingo (UASD), which has 60,000 students. By most standards of judgment, the UASD is woefully underfunded and is too intimately tied up with the nation's political turmoil. During his fifth term from 1986–1990, President Balaguer engaged in budget battles with UASD officials and students who occasionally challenged police in violent demonstrations. These demonstrations were a far cry from the political confrontations of the 1960s, however, when topics such as democracy, human rights, and constitutionalism were the issues of the day, or the protests against the repression of the Balaguer governments in the 1970s, when military units fire indiscriminately at the students to end their protests. Nevertheless, UASD continues to be a center of opposition to the government even though the terms of opposition have changed. Other universities such as the Catholic university in Santiago, Universidad Catolica Madre y Maestra, and the technical university in Santo Domingo, Universidad Nacional Pedro Henriquez Urena, have escaped the tensions present at UASD and, as a result, have developed reputations for more stable learning environments.

The primary reason for the shift from politics to economics in student attitudes in Dominican universities is that the overwhelming majority of the young people come from the middle class. Many of them want to use their education as a means to get ahead and to share in the growing affluence of the country. They are often impatient with or indifferent to politics; seeing the university as an escalator for upward mobility, they have helped depoliticize the campus since the great upheavals in the 1960s.

Still other students remain highly political, and the university is their training ground. The activists are divided between PLD, PRD, and PRSC groups, as well as a number of Communist, Socialist, and far Left factions. The university students, sometimes reinforced by high school students, often constitute the most visible counterforce to governmental power, and they are particularly active against repressive regimes. They serve as national spokespersons on such issues as freedom, democracy, repression, and social justice. Through the Dominican Student Federation (FED), they often keep at center stage political issues that other groups are content to ignore. By themselves, the students cannot topple a government, but they can certainly embarrass one. In alliance with such groups as organized labor and some discontented military officers and elements from the middle class, they have the potential to help lead a radical movement, as in the 1965 revolution.

Except for an occasional budget dispute and the presence of students in the urban violence to protest austerity measures, the inauguration of competitive democracy in 1978 returned the universities to a level of calm. Increasingly, Dominican students recognize the importance of a university education in the fast-changing world economy, particularly with the trade and investment opportunities currently developing in the region. The citizens realize that their universities provide important technical training that the country desperately needs. These schools are also a major and sometimes the last bastion of contrary ideas and a key source of national political leadership. Whatever their problems, academic or political, the universities and their student bodies remain vigilant.

Organized Labor

The Dominican labor movement has had its ups and downs. Suppressed by Trujillo, it emerged as a significant force for the first time in the 1960s. Persecuted again during the period of the revolution and its aftermath and tightly regulated and controlled under Balaguer, the unions have recently begun to make another comeback.

Since the 1960s when there were four major labor groups (Communist, PRD, Social Christian, and that sponsored by the U.S. embassy), the union movement has grown to eight confederations, some still with strong ties to political parties and others controlling specific areas of economic life such as the sugar workers at the Central Romana. The unionized workers in the Dominican Republic number approximately 354,000, although some labor organizers put the number at 500,000. The discrepancy is a reflection of the intense competition among the unions for membership and political influence, which has contributed to their unwillingness to join forces to achieve common goals.[4]

The cutthroat competition among the confederations has left the labor union movement not only divided but also weak and unable to effectively challenge the new working conditions found in the export processing zones or the austerity measures of the government. Unions have few funds, their organizational and training programs are limited, and their leaders are susceptible to employers buying them off or using police to intimidate them. The unemployment rate is so high that employers know they can easily replace workers who seek to unionize. Government restrictions on union activities are so rigid that it is virtually impossible to organize a legal strike in the Dominican Republic.

With a sympathetic social-democratic government installed in the National Palace in 1978, the situation of the unions began to improve. But organized labor is still a comparatively weak force in the Dominican Republic, often intimidated by the military or employers, not able to compete with well-financed company unions, forced to accept sweetheart contracts, and certainly no match for the more powerful employer interests.

The situation of unorganized labor is even more dismal. The large lumpen proletariat of the capital city, as we have seen, lives in miserable conditions with no organization or laws to protect it. Its members formed some of the "shock troops" in the 1965 civil war and the most aggressive demonstrations during the urban unrest in the 1980s and 1990s. Unfortunately, they were also its chief victims.

The rural peasantry—still roughly half the population—is also unorganized and therefore powerless. There are a few farm cooperatives and peasant leagues, but the formation of a strong national peasants' association begun under Bosch was ruled out by his successors. Numerically the country's largest group, the peasantry is simply not a force that counts for much in Dominican national politics.

The U.S. Presence

The United States is a major actor in the Dominican Republic, not just in terms of the country's international trade and relations but in its internal politics as well. It may safely be said that, along with the military and the economic elites, the United States is a major domestic political force—and not necessarily ranked behind them.

There are some 12,000 Americans living and working in the Dominican Republic. This is a small number in comparison with the Dominican population, but it represents an extremely influential group. The Americans are concentrated in banking and commercial concerns, in the hundreds of assembly plants in the free zones, in religious and educational institutions, and in the U.S. embassy. The latter is a major hub of Dominican national politics.

The U.S. government has been deeply involved in Dominican internal affairs at least since the turn of the century. One need only recall the two long military occupations during this period and the almost constant meddling of the United States in Dominican affairs during more "normal" times. Although the U.S. influence has waxed and waned, the Dominican Republic can be thought of as a dependency, a satellite—almost a colony of the United States. Private capital, foreign aid, technical assistance, military training missions, and the long arms of its embassy give the United States a vast range of levers with which to manipulate the Dominican Republic. U.S. officials in the Dominican Republic often act more as proconsuls than as the representatives of one sovereign state to another.

The heavy hand of the United States in the Dominican Republic has, strangely, seldom been the subject of widespread resentment. The U.S. intervention in 1965 generated considerable anti-Americanism, and there is some resentment of U.S. company officials who cluster into compounds with their own exclusive supermarkets and clubs. But many Dominicans continue to look on the United States as a *patrón* and protector, a dispenser of aid and technology—a source of inspiration as well as consternation. Additionally, adept Dominican politicians have learned to manipulate the United States, just as the United States manipulates them.

In recent years, the relations between Dominicans and Americans have suffered some strains. The disclosure in the late 1970s that the Gulf and Western Company reneged on payments to the Dominican government of millions of dollars in sugar futures prompted renewed talk of nationalizing Gulf and Western holdings. Revelations also that the Philip Morris Company bribed members of the Balaguer government did not sit well with the Dominicans. During the administration of Antonio Guzmán and Jorge Blanco, relations between the Dominican Republic and the United States were strained primarily over the drop in sugar quotas, which severely affected foreign earnings and crippled the sugar industry. Since the return of Joaquín Balaguer to the presidency in 1986, Dominican-U.S. relations have entered a period of accommodation and mutual respect. The Caribbean Basin Initiative of the Reagan administration and the Enterprise for the Americas Initiative of President George Bush have been well received in the Dominican Republic and have led to new trade opportunities, along with an increase in U.S. investment. President Balaguer praised the initiative on a number of occasions and lobbied for its extension in 1990. Furthermore, the anguish over the presence of U.S. business in the Dominican Republic has receded. Guzmán, Jorge, and Balaguer pushed for more attractive investment incentives and expanded the industrial zones in spite of reservations by leftists. The Dominicans have also been pursuing a more independent foreign policy recently and seem determined to sever some of their dependency ties with the United States.

But despite the maturing of the relationship with the United States and the lessening of tensions over the corporate presence, the basic facts of life are that the Dominicans are still strongly dependent on the Americans and that the United States maintains a strategic hold on the nation's economic and political life. It is not likely that the United States will quickly relinquish that hold. Realistic Dominicans recognize that fact and adjust accordingly.

What is likely is some modest readjustment of the terms of dependency and of the role of the United States in their country. The United States now has fewer official personnel there and contributes less aid than in the last thirty years; consequently, it has fewer official levers to manipulate. That, however, did not stop the Americans from putting pressure on Balaguer and the military in 1978 to allow the vote count to proceed to a democratic outcome. But though the official U.S. presence has been somewhat diminished, the private one has been increased, in the form of large U.S. multinational corporations. The American presence thus remains a strong one in the Dominican Republic, but the form it takes is different, and, as we shall see, the whole international context in the Caribbean is also undergoing alteration.[5]

* * *

Power in the Dominican Republic remains imbalanced. It is concentrated in the hands of the few, not the many. That was clear in our discussions of both the class and social structure and the relative power of the social and interest groups. A decided inequality of wealth and political strength persists. Clearly the most important groups in internal Dominican politics are the armed forces, the economic elites, and the Americans. Of secondary importance are the church, the students, and the organized labor movement. Of almost no consequence at all, at least politically, are the largest groups numerically: the urban slum dwellers and the peasants. Hence, although the foundations for a more pluralistic and democratic system in the Dominican Republic have been laid, the process of democratization is still in its early stages and remains incomplete.[6]

6

The Economy

The Dominican Republic has always been a country of passionate politics, intense interpersonal relations, and constant preoccupation with class and status issues. But more recently, as the country has modernized, economic issues have come to the fore. One should not go so far as to say economics has replaced politics as the major national preoccupation, but such a statement would not be too far from the truth.

FROM POLITICS TO POLITICAL ECONOMY

In the early 1960s, following Trujillo's death, the Dominican Republic had become a highly politicized nation. There were new parties, new ideologies, new political groups and movements, new policies and international concerns. The country experienced a sudden explosion of political mobilization. This period of high political intensity reached a crescendo in the 1965 revolution.

But since 1965, some dramatic changes have occurred: The country has been depoliticized; ideological and partisan passions have declined; politicians and political programs have yielded center stage to economists, managers, businesspeople, technicians, and economic development plans. The attention of the Dominican people is less on the political divisions of the past than on getting ahead and stimulating further economic growth, for themselves and for the nation.

Economic development is now talked about in passionate terms. Political leaders who once debated intensely over various constitutional clauses, ideologies, and political party programs are now preoccupied with foreign loan opportunities, balance of payments deficits, industrial free zones, and the price of sugar. Moreover, the 1990s have ushered in a new era of international economics. Free trade, regional agreements, and global ties to countries that heretofore were viewed as having little impact on Dominican development have been thrust into the forefront of national policy. This is not to suggest politics has disappeared from the Dominican

Workers shipping sugar cane to the processing mill (*Warren Smith; courtesy of Public Affairs Analysts, Inc.*)

Republic, but it is to say that the economy and all facets of it are becoming the primary focus. The country has come full circle from the intensely political years of the early 1960s. For the moment (a very important qualifier!), the Dominican Republic has put aside some of its earlier political conflicts in favor of a long agenda of economic development priorities. Issues of political economy now command more attention that those of pure politics.

The major objective of the Dominican Republic in this new era is to move away from its earlier status as an underdeveloped, dependent, single-crop economy that relies heavily on export earnings and employment derived from this single crop. In place of this "mono-economy," the Dominicans are working to create an economy in which the sources of income and the modes of production are diversified and control of the country's economic future is more in the hands of the Dominicans themselves, rather than dependent on any single foreign importer, that is, the United States. To that end, the Dominicans are working strenuously to build an economy based on a healthy mixture of light industry, mining, tourism, and a modernized agricultural sector, which together will increase growth, lessen the dependence on sugar, and counter the uncertainty of fluctuating world prices.

The consequences of the Dominican's historical dependence on sugar should be emphasized. Fluctuations in the price of sugar have made and unmade Dominican governments for generations. Because the country is so overwhelmingly dependent on its earnings from sugar, a price drop of as little as a few cents per pound can spell ruin for the Dominican economy.[1] Also, if U.S. sugar beet producers form a powerful lobby to keep out foreign sugar or if the House Agricultural Committee, which sets import quotas, decides to give a higher quota to the Philippines—any of these steps can be disastrous for the Dominicans. Or suppose U.S. consumers decide to drink light beer instead of sugared beer or to use saccharine or other sugar substitutes on their coffee or soft drinks—that can also ruin the Dominican economy. Given such uncertainties and their dependence on markets over which they have no control, the Dominican need to diversify is imperative.

The push for diversification and economic independence will not be easy. The Dominican export dependency also helps perpetuate other dependency relationships. The country must also look to foreign sources for capital, energy, and industrial technology. Without these, the Dominicans cannot hope to modernize. Like many Third World nations, the Dominican Republic is caught between its desire for greater economic independence and its reliance on foreign capital, markets, resources, investment, and technology in order to develop.

Hence, the transition from an underdeveloped, dependent, single-crop economy to a more independent and diversified one will not be immediate. There are both older and newer forms of dependency. Although the Dominicans are seeking to lessen their dependence on sugar, they remain absolutely dependent on outside sources for their petroleum. And though they are seeking to diversify their trade, they are still dependent on foreign markets to sell their products. It is in this context of transition and changing dependency relationships that we will discuss the Dominican economy.

THE EXPORT SECTOR: THE OLD AND THE NEW

To understand the nature of the Dominican economy, one must examine the traditional export sector and the manner in which it influences the present economic situation. The Dominican Republic has been and continues to be a country where agricultural production is the most important sector in terms of employment and output for domestic production. Yet, as a sign of the shifting economic base in the country, agriculture has fallen to second place behind mining as a source of export earnings. In 1989, agriculture produced 15.2 percent of the GDP, generated 44 percent of the non–free zone exports, and directly employed 25 percent

Ferronickel plant at Bonao (*Warren Smith; courtesy of Public Affairs Analysts, Inc.*)

of the labor force. Sugar and sugar by-products remain the driving force behind the Dominican agricultural sector, but they have become less dominant as reductions in U.S. sugar quotas and the introduction of so-called nontraditional agricultural exports such as pineapples and flowers have risen in importance.

Meanwhile, the mining sector has moved to the lead in export volume and revenue. In 1989, this sector accounted for 4.1 percent of the GDP and 47 percent of Dominican exports. The nation's mining sector is quite diverse, with ferronickel, gold, and silver as the principal extractive industries. Fueled by favorable incentives for foreign exploratory investment, mining has become an integral part of the country's attempt to move away from its heavy reliance on agriculture.

Among the critical ingredients in the Dominican export sector are the free zones (sometimes termed export processing zones). Factories in the zones receive tax and other benefits; in return, they provide needed jobs to Dominicans. With nineteen existing zones and more planned, the Dominican Republic has seen the value of exports to the United States from the zones (where 94 percent of the materials brought to the country duty free are reexported after assembly) rise from $205 million in 1985 to $692 million in 1989. Exports from the zones—primarily clothing, electronic equipment, leather goods, textiles, and industrial staples—have turned the Dominican Republic into what some have called a mini Taiwan, with unlimited growth potential. Government officials in the United States anticipate that free zone exports, approaching $850 million in 1990, will head toward the $1 billion mark by 1992.[2]

It is becoming increasingly clear that free zones are the growth area in the Dominican economy. Although agriculture has experienced a mild resurgence as a result of new investment in export-oriented agribusiness ventures, reliance on agriculture and mining (which is also susceptible to the vagaries of the world pricing system) is too risky. The Dominican Republic will continue to modernize agriculture and expand its involvement in the extractive industries, but the free zones seem to hold the key to the future of economic development in the country.

The fact that the Dominican Republic depends so heavily on export revenue and decision made by foreign governments, corporations, and consumers has created a dependent economy that experienced regular balance of trade deficits in recent years. The trade deficit in 1989, for example, was $900 million, an increase of almost $200 million from 1988. the source of the deficit was the high costs of petroleum products, coupled with the poor performance of sugar exports and the extractive industries. The United States continued to be the major trading partner of the Dominican Republic, receiving 68 percent of Dominican exports and providing 50 percent of Dominican imports. Principal U.S. exports to the Dominican Republic are textiles, cereals, petroleum derivatives, and appliances. Principal U.S. imports from the Dominican Republic are garments, gold, sugar, ferronickel, coffee, and cocoa.

In recent years, the Dominican Republic has sought to expand its trading relations by developing closer ties to Japan, Germany, and Spain, along with Latin American countries such as Brazil and Argentina. It recently began more active trading in agricultural commodities with the European Community as a result of the Lome IV Accords, which gave the country greater access to European markets. Yet, despite the movement to diversify trading alliances, the Dominican Republic continues to consider the United States as the major player in its development plans. Whether it be the level of the sugar quota, the interest in nontraditional agricultural commodities, extractive investment, or free zone employment, the Dominican Republic will be inextricably tied to the U.S. economy for the foreseeable future.

THE IMPACT OF TRADE IMBALANCES: DEBT AND DEVALUATION

The yearly declines in export revenues caused by changes in world prices, corporate investment decisions, and policies followed by foreign governments have had a ripple effect on the entire economy. One of the most serious results of the trade imbalance in the Dominican Republic is the rising level of indebtedness. As of 1990, the nation had accumulated an external debt of $4 billion, plus an additional $700 million in arrears due to the unwillingness of the government to dip further into its foreign reserve accounts to meet borrowing obligations. What is most disturbing about the debt is that it currently amounts to 60 percent of the GDP and creates a staggering drain on the economy. If government revenue is channeled to pay for the foreign debt, there is little left for essential services and development initiatives. If the government decides to postpone debt payments, as President Balaguer has done on occasion, then the country is denied new loans and loses the confidence and support of the international banking community. The result is a vicious cycle of indebtedness and decay that can only be remedied by a healthy export economy.[3]

To stimulate the export economy, the Dominican government has followed a program of currency devaluation designed to make Dominican goods more attractive to the external market while also hiking the price of imported goods that contribute to the severe balance of payments crisis. In recent years, the value of the peso has declined vis-à-vis the U.S. dollar from $3.85 in 1987 to over $12 in 1992. The devaluations reflect a significant drop in international reserves. In 1989, for example, international reserves fell $164 million from a level of $254 million, a figure that most economists felt was woefully insufficient. During most of 1990, the level of foreign reserves was barely sufficient to cover one month of imports.

Besides the devaluations, the Dominican government has started unpopular campaigns to crack down on exporters suspected of failing to give the central bank the full proceeds of their export earnings and to limit the amount of foreign travel. All these efforts are designed to attract foreign currency, restrict capital flight, and lessen the trade imbalance that has contributed to a growing debt burden that the Dominican Republic has been unable to address. In the view of foreign economic experts, however, the key to economic restructuring in the Dominican Republic is the exchange rate, which has been kept artificially high due to Balaguer's concern over the political ramifications of devaluation-driven price rises. It is interesting to note that the most significant devaluations occurred after the 1990 elections, and, as expected, they created widespread protest.

ROADBLOCKS TO A SOUND ECONOMY: INFLATION AND UNEMPLOYMENT

Foreign debt and the desperate need for foreign currency are not the only challenges faced by the Dominican economy. Since the late 1980s the

Dominican Republic has been experiencing runaway inflation rates of 40 to 50 percent. The public sector programs of President Balaguer (particularly housing construction) that pumped millions of dollars into the economy to stimulate employment, the unwillingness to deal with an overvalued peso, and the ever-present petroleum costs that skyrocketed during the early days of the Persian Gulf War forced prices upward to levels that Dominicans had rarely seen in the past.

From modest price increases during the Balaguer miracle years (the 1970s) and tolerable rates during the terms of the PRD presidents (1978–1986), the Dominican inflation rate jumped dramatically during the most recent Balaguer administration. In 1987, the first full year of Balaguer's fifth term as president, inflation was 25 percent, but by 1990, at the end of this term, the rate was approaching 50 percent. Some foreign economists believe the rate is actually 60 percent and higher, but because of the way in which the Dominican government computes these rates, the level of inflation appears somewhat less threatening.

Nevertheless, the staggering price increases have made the Balaguer government the target of relentless protest from all sectors of Dominican society. In the fall of 1990, Balaguer was forced to accept a plan that increased minimum wages in return for agreement on the reduction in subsidies of staple commodities. Although this quieted the protesters, it was viewed by many as but a brief interlude in what has become an unending battle to control prices. The Dominican Republic in recent years is a nation that merely fine-tunes its price structure, with wage increases followed by devaluations followed by decreases in government food subsidies followed by renewed clamor for wage increases.

Not only does the Dominican Republic suffer from ever-growing inflation rates, but it has also been unable to reduce an unemployment rate that is mired at the 30-percent range. In recent decades, the country has had to accept the fact that it is unable to meet the employment demands of its growing population. With thousands of new job-seeking Dominicans entering the market yearly, the government has had only limited success in finding untapped sources of employment. The free zones have only made a dent in the unemployment picture, while Balaguer's highly vaunted public works projects have been trimmed in an effort to cut the budget and temper inflation. What is perhaps even more disturbing about the employment picture is the level of unemployment in the rural areas, which some say is nearing 60 percent, and the increased presence of underemployed Dominicans in the major cities. Like many Latin American countries, the Dominican Republic is a nation of too many shoeshine men, cigarette vendors, and other types of peddlers.[4]

Obviously, with such large portions of the population economically inactive, it is impossible to achieve a vigorous revival in spending and growth. Consequently, many Dominicans have given up looking for work in their country and instead have decided to take their chances in Puerto Rico or New York City, where opportunities may be more available. This exportation of workers has, in a strange way, created a foreign reserve bonanza as Dominicans in Puerto Rico and the United States send home an estimated $800 million yearly in remittances. For a government desperate for foreign exchange, the transfer of workers to Puerto Rico and the United States is quietly viewed as one attractive solution to the unemployment problem.

GOVERNMENT PROGRAMS TO STRENGTHEN THE ECONOMY

The Dominican effort to redefine, restructure, and reform its present condition of economic underdevelopment and dependency is an enormous, some would say impossible, task. The significant achievements of a more diversified economy and new trade arrangements have been more than offset by the burgeoning costs of OPEC oil and the continued depressed price of many commodities. Rather than diminishing or disappearing as the country modernizes and rearranges its trade relationships, dependency seems only to take on new forms. The desire to transform the economy is thus fraught with disappointment and frustration. Change is slow and often imperceptible; many features of the Dominican vicious circles of underdevelopment seem immune to change.

Yet the Dominicans are unified in their desire to take the necessary steps to expand trade, stimulate diversification, reduce underdevelopment, increase investments, control oil-price-related inflation, and expand the country's economic base. To achieve both greater independence and modernization, the Dominican government has undertaken a number of initiatives.

Trimming Budgets and Privatization

Many of those who have studied the Dominican economy agree that if the country is to enter a new period of growth and price stability, it must get its own house in order. Two critical objectives are cutting public sector budgets and moving toward a privatization of state enterprises. The Dominicans are now well aware of the term *austerity*, as both the PRD presidents and Balaguer have sought to rein in the huge outlays for the public sector.

President Balaguer has been reluctant to reduce government spending primarily because he views it as a stimulus to growth. In particular, the period before the 1990 election was one of significant public sector spending on dams, bridges, housing, and the Columbus lighthouse, which is to be the landmark of the 1992 celebrations. After winning the election, Balaguer was convinced by international lending agencies and Central Bank officials to refrain from using the public sector as an engine of growth because this contributed to hyperinflation and was out of line with current trends in the region to reduce deficits. As a result, Balaguer cut the public sector deficit from 6.2 percent of the GDP in 1988 to 4.5 percent in 1990.

This budget reduction process has not been accomplished without pain and protest, as traditional government subsidies, social welfare benefits, and wages are reduced or delayed. Balaguer has had to face embarrassing strikes from doctors and teachers angry over reductions in pay and other work-related benefits. Moreover, the heavy dependence on public sector employment has declined as the government shifts toward encouraging private investment and development as the keys to job expansion. Although the Dominican Republic still relies heavily on the public sector for employment and economic stimulus, it no longer sees government as the only answer to development.

Nowhere is this reduction in government spending and visibility more evident than in efforts by the Dominicans to begin the process of privatization. With huge state-owned enterprises left over from the Trujillo era and those developed in the heyday of state capitalism during the 1960s and 1970s, the Dominican Republic had placed key industries such as sugar, electricity, and cement in the hands of government officials. In the 1990s, however, the Dominicans are following the trend, now widespread throughout Latin America, of selling these sectors to private investors, even if those investors are from outside the country. Because privatization requires scaling back the role of the government and thus its patronage and contract opportunities, the process of privatization has been slow in the Dominican Republic. But at the same time, the need for efficient agriculture and industry, along with a reduction in public sector outlays for wasteful state-run enterprises, has prompted the Balaguer government to begin efforts at privatization. Clearly, privatization is being viewed in the Dominican Republic as one way to transform the face of government.

Promoting Exports and Attracting Foreign Investment

While the Dominican government is actively working to reduce its role in the economy and shift the emphasis to the private sector, it is also aggressively pursuing potential export opportunities and seeking foreign investment.[5] A government agency, the Dominican Center for the Promotion of Exports (CEDOPEX) has been created to aid local businesses seeking expanded markets for their products and to work with interested companies in the United States that want to benefit from the free zones or other sector possibilities. CEDOPEX provides three major services: (1)

training programs to assist Dominican businesspeople in gaining access to foreign markets, (2) market research to determine the potential for sales of goods in foreign countries, and (3) information and guidance to prospective investors that will ease the process of entering the Dominican economy. CEDOPEX maintains offices in New York, the Caribbean, and Latin America.

CEDOPEX also is part of a growing list of public and private agencies that are working to either gain access to U.S. markets or to attract foreign investment. The Investment Promotion Council, with offices in Santo Domingo, provides information and videos to businesses interested in locating in the Dominican Republic. The American Chamber of Commerce of the Dominican Republic, in the Hotel Santo Domingo, has for years been a staunch ally of the Dominican government's effort to promote investment in the country. A recent addition to this export promotion and investment group is the Joint Agribusiness Coinvestment Council (JACC), which seeks to work with foreign businesses interested in benefiting from the Dominican Republic's program to move away from sugar to a wider range of nontraditional agricultural products. The JACC has matching funds available to help finance agribusiness feasibility studies. Finally, the United States Commerce Department is active in working with U.S. firms that want to enter the Dominican Republic, writing regular reports and conducting seminars to inform businesspeople on the most efficient way to accomplish this.

Along with export promotion and the investment agencies, the Dominican Republic has formulated a number of investment incentive laws designed to attract foreign capital and technology. The basic legislation governing all foreign investment is Law No. 861, which grants foreign investors the right to remit capital and profits and exchange local currency. Although the profit remittance issue has been a source of confusion and disagreement over the years, it has not been a barrier to continued business interest in the Dominican Republic. Joining Law No. 861 is the Industrial Incentive Law (Law No. 299), which provides generous income tax and import duty exemptions of 100 percent on a series of classified enterprises (see Table 6.1).

These two key pieces of legislation are among a number of laws providing incentives to foreign investors in the exportation of nontraditional agricultural products, mining, and tourism. Together, these laws are part of a growing system of legislation and government agencies that seek to attract foreign investment and thus speed up the transformation of the Dominican economy. Although there are some areas of the economy that are protected from foreign investment and there are additional restrictions on foreign ownership and joint ventures, the Dominican government has been quite flexible in accommodating businesses from outside the country

TABLE 6.1   Law No. 299: Incentives for Investment

Incentives Offered	Industrial Categories		
	A	B	C
Exemption from import duties and taxes on raw materials, semi-finished products, or materials used in the composition or processing of the product, container, or packing material	100%	95%	Up to 90%
Exemption from import duties and taxes on machinery and equipment	100%	—	—
Exemption from import duties and taxes on fuels and lubricants used strictly for industrial processing, except gasoline	100%	95%	Up to 90%
Exemption from income tax	100%	Up to 50% on investments	Up to 50% on investments

Definition of Categories

For the purpose of granting the benefits and concessions provided by Law No. 299, industrial activities have been classified in the three categories designated A, B, and C.

A Industries engaged in the manufacture of products for the export market only. Assembly plants fall into this category.

B All new industries of high priority to national development, especially those engaged in the manufacture of items not produced in the country that are intended to replace imported products, satisfying a demand of the domestic market.

C All new production or expansion of existing industries engaged in the processing of local raw materials or in the manufacture of products for domestic consumption.

Class A, B, and C industries enjoy the benefits of their classification for the period of time indicated below in accordance with their geographical location. Twenty-year concessions are usually granted to Class A industries regardless of location.

Santo Domingo	8 years
Santiago	10 years
frontier zone	20 years
anywhere else in the country	15 years

and is working to cut through much of the red tape that has, in the past, hindered the entry of new investment into the economy.

The efforts of the Dominican Republic to attract foreign investment both brought aggressive marketing and positive legislative initiatives have led to a steady increase in investor interest. The heaviest foreign investment has been in the agricultural and foodstuffs sector, but there also have been noticeable increases in mining, finance, tourism, and, of course, light industrial assembly. Total foreign investment in the Dominican Republic in 1989 was over $600 million, with the United States contributing about 47 percent of this total. The Balaguer government, in particular, has worked diligently to create a proinvestment climate in the Dominican Republic, which is described by U.S. Department of Commerce officials as a country that "supports and encourages private investment."

Expanding Tourism

Tourism is one area of economic life in which the Dominican Republic hopes to achieve long-term success. The nation is now being touted as the "best-kept secret in the Caribbean." The Dominican Republic had just 67,000 tourists in 1970, but it welcomed over 1 million visitors in 1989 and now boasts the largest number of hotel rooms in the Caribbean, with over 17,000. This number is expected to climb to 22,000 by the 1992 celebrations. More importantly, tourism is now the number one source of foreign exchange, garnering US$568 million in 1987.[6]

The foreign exchange benefits derived from the arrival of so many Americans and Europeans is only part of the success of tourism. For thousands of impoverished Dominicans, tourism also means lobs as baggage handlers, cab drivers, maids, waiters, groundskeepers, and so forth. These are often demeaning and not very high-paying jobs, but they are certainly better than no jobs at all.

To monitor the tourist industry and plan its growth, the government has developed the Department of Tourist Investment and Infrastructure (INFRATUR), a Central Bank agency that is charged with investing in tourist-related infrastructure such as roads, sewers, water systems, and airports. The government also has a very visible tourist information system, with offices in New York, Toronto, Montreal, and in Dominican embassies in Europe and Latin America. The government is dedicated to expanding its tourist sector not only in terms of promotion but also in terms of construction incentives. For a period of ten years, the Tourist Incentive Law provides 100 percent income tax exemption, exoneration from construction taxes, taxes on incorporation or capital increases, and municipal taxes on licenses, and 100 percent relief from import duties.

The Dominicans are well aware that the tourist dollar, mark, or frank is subject to the whims of the consumer, but with the continued stability of Dominican democracy, a friendly populace, few if any instances of terrorism, and, most importantly, some of the most gorgeous beaches in the world, the Dominican Republic is a fresh and virtually untouched paradise. Government leaders are banking on the "discovery" of the country in 1992 as a bonanza that will generate hundreds of millions of dollars in foreign currency and allow them to further diversify their economy.

Beach at Playa Dorada on the north coast (*courtesy of the Dominican Republic Tourism Promotion Council*)

Working with the International Community

Dominicans increasingly feel they must control and direct their own development process, yet the government also recognizes that it must form a close working arrangement with international lending organizations, retain the confidence of commercial sources of credit, and ensure that foreign assistance ties are not jeopardized. As the economy in the Dominican Republic continues to falter, there is little prospect that attaining a semblance of stability and steady growth can be achieved without considerable help from external sources.[7]

Although Dominican leaders realize that foreign loans and grants are essential for the economy, there has been great reluctance, if not anger, among the general populace about becoming ensnarled in the restructuring proposals that often accompany assistance from international lending agencies such as the IMF. The agreement reached between the Jorge government and the IMF in the mid-1980s precipitated one of the worst bouts of urban violence in the nation's history. Since that agreement (which many outside observers feel had a positive impact on the Dominican economy, despite the sacrifice and reforms that it mandated), Dominican political leaders have been hesitant to approach the IMF for additional support, fearing popular repercussions of the austerity measures that would be called for.

The Balaguer government has reopened negotiations with the International Monetary Fund to address the Dominicans' outstanding debt problem and ensure the continued flow of development loans. But ever-conscious of the negative response that working with the IMF brings in the Dominican Republic, Balaguer has tried to calm the citizenry by stating that the foreign debt would be paid "only within the country's means" and would not impose heavy adjustment conditions. Despite these bold announcements, those within governing circles in the Dominican Republic realize that without IMF assistance the Dominican economy would slide further into decline and, even worse, would be less capable of attracting future loans.

The negotiations with the IMF are viewed as critical to the rescheduling of commercial bank obligations and bilateral loan arrangements. As of 1990, 22 percent of Dominican external debt is owed to commercial banks, and 34 percent is in the form of bilateral loans to advanced industrial nations, often termed the Paris Club. The remaining debt is owed to countries such as Mexico and Venezuela, which have signed oil agreements with the Dominican Republic, and multilateral lending organizations such as the Inter-American Development Bank and the World Bank.

The dependence of the Dominican Republic on external assistance has become an important part of its development program. Total disbursements of donor assistance to the nation amounted to $157 million in 1989, which was up from $84.7 million in 1988. This total is broken down into (1) multilateral donors such as the World Bank, which contributed $31.8 million in 1989, the Inter-American Development Bank, which contributed $53.4 million, the United Nations, $6.8 million, and the European Economic Community, $4.1 million, and (2) bilateral donors such as the United States, which contributed $32 million, Italy, $20.5 million, and Japan, $3.7 million, along with Germany, France, and Korea, which contributed lesser amounts.

The foreign assistance of the United States, traditionally the largest bilateral aid provider to the Dominican Republic, dropped dramatically during the second term of Ronald Reagan and during the presidency of George Bush. After Reagan consistently allocated over $100 million to the Dominican Republic during the heyday of the Caribbean Basin Initiative, the realities of shrinking budgets and diminished attention to the region after the end of the Sandinista regime brought the aid dollars down to the range of $25–35 million.[8] The Dominicans, who feel that political stability, successful democratization, and consistent cooperation with the United States should be rewarded, have been distressed over Washington's failure to support an ally, especially an ally that is so close to U.S. borders and has such a wide range of economic and human ties.

THE FUTURE OF THE DOMINICAN ECONOMY

Speculating on any nation's future economic development is risky. This is especially so in the Dominican case, with its history of political ups and downs and an economy subject to unpredictable and uncontrollable external forces. Caution and balance are required.

Few in the Dominican Republic now think that the country can again match its miracle growth rates of the early to mid-1970s; oil price increases and the depressed state of commodity prices largely rule that out. Yet the Dominican economy and people have shown a remarkable resistance to adversity. Despite continued existence as a small and dependent nation, despite natural calamity, and despite immense social and economic problems, the Dominican economy is showing renewed vitality. Agricultural production increased by the late 1980s, foreign investment continues to flow in, imports have leveled off, tourism is booming, and the economy is less and less dependent on King Sugar.

Looking at the price of petroleum, the high unemployment, the balance of payments deficits, the debt obligations, and the structural weaknesses in the economy, a pessimistic outlook on the economic future of the Dominican Republic is understandable. Yet, despite the seemingly endless list of obstacles to development and economic stability, many

Dominicans see signs of opportunity amidst the roadblocks. Whatever optimism can be found in the Dominican Republic comes from the hope that the move toward privatization, access to the U.S. market, new ties to Europe and the Pacific Basin, and the continued boom in free zones and tourism will begin to slowly bring the country into a more prosperous era.

Much of the optimism hinges on how these radical experiments in downsizing the public sector and forming new trading alliances turn out. It is one thing to talk about the miracle of the marketplace and the wonders of free trade, but it is another to successfully bring about the transition from a state-dominated economy to one that is highly competitive and efficient. National leadership will also play a significant role in the future of the economy. With Balaguer as president, the country has been headed by a leader who has clearly lost his image as the master administrator and guarantor of normalcy. With his departure, the Dominican Republic could once again be swept up in a political tangle that would cast doubt on the government's ability to deal with the economy or attract support from the external sector.

Nevertheless, there are some hopeful signs for the Dominican economy. The prospect of having a free trade zone that encompasses the Western Hemisphere (as President Bush suggested) could energize the region. The extension of the Caribbean Basin Initiative points to the confidence that the United States has in the region as a potential counterweight to the Pacific Rim. The arrival of the European Community in 1992, with its accent on open borders, is already reaping benefits for the Dominican Republic in terms of agricultural exports and is expected to increase economic opportunities. And the fact that the Dominican Republic has already become home to a number of multinational corporations and has gained a reputation for having a positive work environment will position it well for the onset of the global economy.

As in much of the Third World, the Dominican Republic must walk a tightrope. The margin for error is small; disaster looms if the tightrope walker loses balance. Yet in the Dominican case, one cannot help but be impressed by the mood of confidence and determination, by the commitment to democracy, by the assurance, even after so many setbacks, that the nation will, in fact, achieve economic modernization, some measure of independence, and that place in the sun to which it has always aspired.

7
Political Institutions
and Processes

If the economy is the lifeblood of the Dominican Republic, then politics can be viewed as its "soul," the very essence of what is Dominican. Both must be cared for and nourished for survival. The Dominican people today clearly understand the influence that sugar prices, inflation, and international markets have on their national life; but it is politics, leadership, the contest for national power that fires their imagination, calls them to action, and defines their world.

Politics in the Dominican Republic is serious business. It is more than a mechanical process of placing people in office to make routine decisions. To the Dominicans, politics provides a forum where the most basic issues of national life are debated and often fought over. Politics is not a campaign merely of competing programs and public relations efforts but a life-and-death struggle to establish certain principles or obtain a preferred and advantageous system of governance. The stakes are high: immense power, position, and status for those who achieve the presidency or ride the president's coattails into office; opportunities for jobs, sinecures, and private enrichment that go with high office; and the prestige and strength that accompany capture of the very pinnacles of the Dominican system. Because the stakes are high, the competition is fierce and frequently violent. Unlike many of the advanced industrial democracies, where alternations in power are routinely accepted and cause little discord, the Dominican Republic continues to reveal deep-seated disagreements over the shape and direction of politics and government administration.

THE TENSION OF COMPETING POLITICAL PHILOSOPHIES

At the heart of Dominican politics lies the conflict between those who believe the country must be governed by an authoritarian and elite-dominated system and those who believe in greater freedom and democracy.

Like many of its sister republics in Latin America, the Dominican political system derived substantially from the Spanish system of centralized authority, hierarchy, order, discipline, and rule from the top down. These traditions have been reinforced by the Dominicans' own history of disorder, revolt, underdevelopment, repeated foreign invasions, and lack of strong institutions. It is argued that only authoritarian rule, iron-clad discipline, and government emanating from the top down, not from the bottom up, can secure the order and stability necessary for development, preventing chaos, repelling foreign threats, and holding together a country that tends toward fragmentation and breakdown.

Authoritarianism went virtually unchallenged during the three centuries of Spanish domination and the ensuing decades of Haitian control. But when the Dominicans gained their independence in 1844, liberalism and republicanism became the ideals. The liberal tenets included limited government, human rights, and free elections.[1]

The competition between the authoritarian and the liberal currents formed the backdrop for much of the Dominican conflict in the nineteenth and twentieth centuries. The liberal Duarte was replaced by the twin authoritarians, Báez and Santana. The next short-lived liberal regime led to the dictatorship of Heureaux. The chaos and anarchy that followed his assassination led first to an occupation by the U.S. Marines and then to Trujillo.

The Trujillo regime carried the authoritarian tradition to its extreme: full-fledged totalitarianism. Heureaux and Trujillo also came closest to resurrecting the still-venerated sixteenth-century Spanish model of a centralized unitary regime, though both went too far and were eventually killed for their excesses. Both sought to eliminate the competing liberal current.

With Trujillo's death in 1961, the competition between these two philosophies of governance was renewed with vigor. The Dominican Republic became a major battleground between liberals and liberalism's skeptics. The chronology is familiar: first a conservative Council of State; then the liberal regime of Juan Bosch, which was promptly overthrown; back to conservative rule; then the revolution, civil war, and U.S. intervention of 1965; again, conservative rule under Balaguer; social democracy under the PRD presidents, Guzmán and Jorge; and back to conservative rule under Balaguer.

Despite the fact that the authoritarian tradition in the Dominican Republic has been gradually weakened and the liberal one slowly strengthened, it would be inaccurate to say the Dominicans have reached a consensus on their political system. There is still too much disagreement

Antonio Guzmán, president from 1978 to 1982 (*courtesy of Jacques Lowe*)

Salvador Jorge Blanco, president from 1982 to 1986 (*courtesy of the Dominican government*)

Joaquín Balaguer Ricardo, president from 1966 to 1978 and from 1986 to the present (*courtesy of the Dominican government*)

Palacio Nacional, the seat of government (*courtesy of the Dominican government*)

over ultimate goals to make such a judgment. The liberal current seems to be gaining, but it could be snuffed out again quite easily. The Joaquín Balaguer in the National Palace in the 1990s is a far different politician than the post–civil war practitioner—resulting in a situation that may be characterized as democracy masking an authoritarian facade. Balaguer performs his role as the democratically elected president in a manner similar to that of his PRD predecessors. There is a growing respect for the institutions of democratic governance and a willingness to allow the free flow of ideas to influence the policy debate. Yet, despite these encouraging signs of change, there are also disturbing signs that the political leadership is isolated from the people, too often willing to use harsh measures to maintain order, and not beyond employing questionable electoral and political maneuvers to control leftist opposition.[2]

Two additional points deserve mention. The first has to do with the values of the younger generation now coming to power and of a larger and more affluent middle class and whether these signal a long-term strengthening of the liberal tradition. We do not know what the precise implications of these changes will be, but we do know the members of the younger generation are often more liberal and open to new ideas than their more authoritarian elders and that sizable portions of the emerging middle class have a strong interest in both stability and democracy. At some time in the future, however, the middle-class values of stability and democracy are likely to prove incompatible, and Dominicans will have to choose between them.

The other point is that since the civil war, a third current of thought, generally categorized as socialism, has been an integral part of the Dominican ideological landscape. Leaders such as Juan Bosch and José Francisco Peña Gómez have dedicated their careers to advancing the Socialist agenda in Dominican politics. In the 1990s, with socialism descredited not only in Eastern Europe but also throughout Latin America, Socialist doctrine as an alternative to authoritarianism and liberal democracy has been abandoned by politicians as a means of rousing the electorate and charting a public policy course for the future. Both Bosch and Peña Gómez have toned down their Socialist rhetoric in the 1990 presidential campaign, and Bosch's call to challenge the Balaguer victory with massive street demonstrations fell on deaf ears. At present, socialism as a third way in Dominican politics is dormant, but that does not mean that it is dead. Deep-seated class divisions and growing disenchantment with democracy could easily resuscitate Socialist values in the future. In the short term, however, socialism no longer attracts many Dominicans. Even most young people, who have been the targets of leftist recruitment, are pleased with the transition from authoritarianism to democracy and hopeful that elections and greater respect for human rights will provide the direction for sustained national development.

THE RULES OF THE GAME

The heritage of disagreement, struggle, and conflict that has so strongly dominated Dominican politics has helped foster a set of operating rules and requirements for participation, leadership, and policymaking. A central tenet has been that politics is a "zero-sum game." The total social and economic product has historically been more or less fixed, so that if one person or group wins, another must lose. Dominican politics is thus a winner-take-all proposition in which virtually any tactics may be used to get to power and stay there.

This implies that a government in power usually treats its opponents as traitors, while the opposition usually views the government as, at best, usurpers. Opposition groups must practice the politics of patient survival for the government often uses repression and intimidation against them. To be an oppositionist requires perseverance, bravery, and ingenuity. The proposition that governs the relations between government and opposition is usually: "Winner takes all, loser takes survival."

Dominican history contains numerous examples of these prevailing patterns. Most often, it has been the advocates of authoritarian rule who have "taken all," and it has been the democrats who have been forced to take "survival." Even a political party like the PRD, which was one of the "out" groups for years, did not show much willingness to involve the opposition in decisionmaking or share with it the spoils of power when it won the presidency in 1978 and in 1982. If progress has been made in the Dominican Republic, it may have emerged in the 1990 election in which Balaguer won the presidency in a disputed vote count, but Bosch and his PLD gained controlled of the Chamber of Deputies, thus, at least on surface, moving the Dominican political system away from the practice of winner take all, loser take survival. Balaguer still controls the key levers of power and patronage, but in the current political arena, institutional competition has become a reality.

But though the survivalist politics of the 1960s and 1970s have been modified as democracy gains a foothold in the Dominican Republic, the election of Joaquín Balaguer in 1986 and his reelection in 1990 brought back a familiar set of rules that now govern Dominican politics. Where the PRD presidents, Guzmán and Jorge, introduced the practices of executive-legislative cooperation, a broad-based advisory system, and a more open policy process, Balaguer's return to power brought back the era of centralized rule, a narrow and poorly respected coterie of personal advisers, and patronage.[3]

In the Dominican Republic of the 1990s, although the nation has clearly strengthened its democratic foundation and created a vibrant political system of competition and opposition, the top political leader has reintroduced a managerial style that is no longer in sync with the rest of the system. Balaguer has, in a real sense, reinvented the practice of joining democratic form with authoritarian practice to meet the changing character of politics in the new era of popular rule. Though legislatures are more important and do challenge the initiatives of the executive, Balaguer continues to be a lone figure working in the middle of the night on even the smallest detail of governance; though opposition political parties work freely with little interference, Balaguer has won two contested elections that were filled with irregularities; and though there is pride that the Dominican Republic has shed its image as a tradition-bound nation with a new and vigorous leadership elite, the eighty-three-year-old president operates as a nineteenth-century caudillo handing out favors, solving problems on a paternalistic basis, and taking complete personal responsibility for the success and failures of his country.

The Dominican Republic may be moving step by step toward a modern democracy of strong institutions, legitimate elections, and pluralistic decisionmaking processes, but it is doing so with a leader who is more comfortable in a much different, earlier tradition. The old adage that the more things change, the more they stay the same may be an appropriate description of the Dominican Republic in the sixth presidency of Joaquín Balaguer.

THE CHARACTER OF LEADERSHIP

The preceding analysis of Joaquín Balaguer points to the importance of presidential leadership in Dominican politics. The president (any president) is the hub and center of the system. If he does well, the country will likely thrive; if he is a disaster, the country can as easily slide downhill. The president has a responsibility, in a personal sense, for both the direction of the collective national life and the well-being of individual citizens.

Dominican politics rests almost exclusively on the quality of personal presidential leadership. From the time of Duarte, the "dual caudillos," and Heureaux through Trujillo, Bosch, and Balaguer, the country has been shaped not so much by formal constitutional arrangements and institutional arrangements but rather by the talents, *personalismo*, charisma, strength, and machismo of the individuals who occupied the National Palace.

The Dominican political system, as in other countries of Latin America, is organized in highly personalistic terms, and its processes of policymaking are seen as the direct responsibility of the president. But through government in most of the other Latin American countries has become increasingly bureaucratic and institutionalized in recent decades, this is far less true in the Dominican Republic. The president makes all decisions, passes on all appointments, holds all the reins in his hands. He is not only the central figure in the hierarchy, he is also largely alone. The president formulates proposals, introduces them to the people, sees that they are enacted, monitors their implementation, and, of course, claims all credit for their success.

The centrality and singularity of executive leadership implies a set of personal qualities necessary for effective management of the government and survival in an often hostile and competitive environment. The Dominican leaders who may have had the most influence on the shape and direction of the country—Heureaux, Trujillo, Balaguer—all possessed similar leadership characteristics. All three governed as authoritarians and sought to present themselves as builders and modernizers, as men who provided unity and constructive progress in a nation that had previously been divided and lacked development. Despite the fact that, in all three cases, development projects were limited largely to infrastructure building rather than providing more basic human services, these leaders were masters of public relations and effectively presented themselves as strong presidents of a nation on the move.

The sense of movement and dynamism generated by Heureaux, Trujillo, and Balaguer was linked to the use of repression against those who criticized them or their policies. They viewed their own power as supreme and uncontestable; those who challenged that premise were viewed as enemies and treated as such.

The outside observer might marvel at the resilience and longevity of the three presidents (Heureaux was in power seventeen years, Trujillo thirty-one, and Balaguer is now in his sixth presidency). The reason for their long terms in office cannot be ascribed simply to repression. All three presidents were shrewd manipulators, paternalistic benefactors, providers of various goods and services, and national guardians who could garner public support even while ruling in an autocratic and often bloody fashion.

Ruling as manipulators, authoritarians, providers, and guardians, all three created around them an aura of benevolence and father-like concern. In varying degrees and with varying styles, they seemed willing to listen to all citizens complaints and to resolve even the most trivial problems. This was done on a highly personal and individual basis; *organized* opposition or complaints were not permitted. Although all three were eventually revealed as power-hungry and self-serving, there is no doubt their rule was based on more than merely a police-state apparatus. Each of them retained his popularity for a long period, with Balaguer still controlling the reins of power. Hence, to many aspiring Dominican politicians, the Heureaux-Trujillo-Balaguer model remains attractive.

Authoritarian leadership in the Dominican Republic seems to require a talent for public relations, a willingness to use force, and a knack for paternalistic control. But it is essential to recognize that some Dominican presidents have viewed their roles differently and practiced a presidential style quite unlike that pattern. Ulises Espaillat, Ramón Cáceres, Juan Bosch, Antonio Guzmán, and Salvador Jorge Blanco stand out as leaders who were committed to the principles of democratic rule and who utilized democratic precepts as the basis for government.

Because of the different time periods in which they ruled and the changing social bases of their power, making generalizations about these democratic presidents is difficult, yet it is possible to distinguish them rather sharply from the authoritarians. These rulers entered office as political reformers. All were determined to change the system. All encouraged reform and greater participation, and they were committed to respect for basic freedoms and democratic politics. All repudiated their autocratic predecessors. And finally, they all had visions of changing the political-economic order, even though they faced enormous obstacles from entrenched elites and generations of tradition.

Their short terms in office compared with those of the authoritarians, their inability to deal with the needs of their constituency, and, in the case of Guzmán and Jorge, their involvement in corruption scandals have led many Dominicans to dismiss these men and their brief experiments with democracy in the Dominican Republic as failures. Yet it cannot be ignored that while they ruled, human rights were respected, democratic freedoms prevailed, reforms were carried out, and the democratic presidents themselves enjoyed widespread support. The accomplishments of the democratic leaders have been limited, but they should not be belittled; in fact, their limited success kept democratic governance as an option in Dominican politics and intensified the pressure for moving the nation away from its authoritarian roots.

What is perhaps most important about the legacy of the democratic leaders is that it has forced a modern authoritarian president like Joaquín Balaguer to function in a new political environment that is gradually becoming institutionalized and requiring more accountability from its politicians. As democracy becomes the accepted mode of governance in the Dominican Republic, Balaguer, who has run the country in a largely nondemocratic manner, has come to recognize that he cannot ignore popular pressures or administer the country as if it were a privately owned business. Even the wily Balaguer has had to accede to public pressure over issues such as negotiations with the IMF, minimum wage disputes, and the process of privatization. What is more, Balaguer has had to ensure that the military and the national police do not exceed their legal mandates for maintaining public order.

But though democratic leaders continue to change politics in the Dominican Republic, they are also undergoing intense scrutiny and criticism, particularly with respect to the issue of public corruption. The use of government employment for illegal personal advantage is nothing new in the Dominican Republic, especially in a country where Trujillo pilfered the treasury for his own gain. But the victory of Antonio Guzmán in 1978 ushered in a new era of expectations in Dominican politics. When he committed suicide over allegations of corruption and when Jorge Blanco left office under the cloud of a military contracting scandal, the Dominican electorate began to sour on civilian politicians and, in the process, question whether democratic politics was capable of changing past practices. Although Balaguer ran on a platform of honesty in 1986, by 1990 even he was being criticized for tolerating drug-related corruption in the armed forces and excessive spending on projects related to the 1992 celebrations.

Today, Dominican politicians must always be conscious that their policies and actions may stir up controversy and limit their capacity to govern. Balaguer, who is more of a father figure than a democratic politician, must be ever-vigilant for challenges to his authority. Because Dominican democracy is still in its infancy, the tightrope brand of leadership can be expected to continue for some time. Leaders will function in an atmosphere where caution, conflict, and survival are the key watchwords of governance.

THE CONTEST FOR POWER

Although politics in the Dominican Republic is often shaped and defined by competition between rival "men-on-horseback" and their retinues, rival personalities and governing styles, and rival philosophical traditions, the system is more complex than that. Politics also takes the form of "ins" versus "outs" (blues versus reds, as they were called historically), factional fights and quarrels, and, above all, wholly different conceptions on the part of distinct groups, pertaining to quite different historical epochs and life-styles, as to the proper shape and direction of the national life.

Since the 1960s, the "in" group has been a coalition of conservative interests led by Joaquín Balaguer, while the "out" group has consisted of a more ill-defined coalition of liberal-democratic or social-democratic interests led by Juan Bosch (until he resigned and formed his own party) and the Dominican Revolutionary Party. To some, this contest has been reduced to a simpler contest between two rival modern-day caudillos, Bosch and Balaguer; but in reality, the division goes deeper than that. It involves a contest between two rival "families," one conservative and traditional in its political preferences and the other modern and change-oriented. This basic split lies at the heart of Dominican politics and helps account for its tensions, conflict, and frequent resort to violence.

The players in this contest have not changed substantially since the assassination of Trujillo. On the one side are the major landowners, business interests, military officers, high church officials, some elements of the emerging middle class, and usually the U.S. embassy. These are the more conservative or status quo-oriented elements or those who favor change but only within the parameters of the existing system. They are led, as they have been generally since the early 1960s, by Joaquín Balaguer. Balaguer successfully separated his support and leadership style from that of Trujillo, offering a somewhat more tolerant attitude toward dissent and organized opposition while continuing to rule in an authoritarian and conservative fashion. This group represents what might be called the "family of order."

Balaguer's supporters never developed a cohesive or ideologically well-defined party organization. For elective purposes and to give the outside world (especially the United States) the impression of an emerging party system in the Dominican Republic, they formed the Partido Reformista (PR), or Reformist Party. But this party consisted chiefly of the personal followers and retinue of Balaguer, and it had no real programmatic or ideological basis. It served as the reelection vehicle for Balaguer and as a giant national patronage and spoils agency, but it never developed as a modern political party organization. Prior to the 1986 election, in what was viewed by many in the Dominican Republic as a brilliant political move, Balaguer joined the PR with the highly respected Social Christian Party to form the Christian Social Reformist Party (PRSC). Balaguer not only gained a new electoral ally but also brought a strong organization and higher level of legitimacy to his candidacy.[4]

Since the PRSC was formed, little has changed in Balaguer's control of party politics, but then Balaguer did not need a strong party organization to bolster his presidency or ensure his reelection. He presents himself and his regime as "traditionally Dominican," above partisan politics, a national unity movement, rather than divisively party-based. Balaguer is a more modern caudillo who, though supported by the same coalition of interests as Trujillo, has proven that conservative objectives could be realized without resort to extensive and brutal repression.

Where Balaguer represents the "ins" and the forces for the status quo, Juan Bosch and his Dominican Liberation Party speak for the "outs," the traditionally forgotten elements in Dominican society. Founded in the 1970s after a dispute with the major opposition party (the PRD), the PLD is, in many respects, Juan Bosch's vehicle for regaining power in the Dominican Republic. Although the PLD has developed a stronger and broader-based organization in recent years (and moved away somewhat from its image as the bastion of radical students and workers), Bosch is still identified as the essence of the PLD and the sole reason for its existence.[5]

It is possible to criticize the personalistic character of the PLD, but one cannot ignore the phenomenal success that the party has had since 1978 in convincing the Dominican electorate that it is the alternative to Balaguer and the "ins." Its steady increases in support in the 1982 and 1986 elections allowed Bosch to make a strong run for the presidency in 1990. However, his defeat by Balaguer appeared to weaken the PLD as party leaders seemed to tire of their leader's emotionalism and public gaffes. At one point in 1991, Bosch left the PLD only to rejoin it, which suggested turmoil in the organization. As to its participation in future elections, the PLD may be forced to come to grips with the issue of whether it is a personalistic party catering to the aspirations of Juan Bosch or whether it is a more institutional party that can continue to participate in politics no matter what happens to its founder. For now, though, the PLD and Bosch seem content to stir up public opposition against Balaguer by staging national strikes and mounting regular challenges to the government's authority.

While the PLD was enjoying a period of popularity and organizational strength, the Dominican Revolutionary Party, which had been the opposition standard-bearer for years and had controlled the presidency from 1978 to 1986, was in the midst of an internal crisis that continues even today. The PRD is one of the earliest social-democratic reform parties in Latin America, with a proud heritage of opposition to the Trujillo dictatorship and development of democracy in the Dominican Republic. Although the party languished in the late 1960s and 1970s under the authoritarian rule of Balaguer and eventually saw its leader, Juan Bosch, leave to form his own party, the troubles in the PRD really began once it moved into power with the election of Antonio Guzmán in 1978.[6]

On taking power, the PRD quickly became the focus of patronage demands by its supporters and the subject of criticism from those who expected quick and significant reform. Leftists within the party, such as José Francisco Peña Gómez, lamented the inadequate social programs of the government and urged faster and more vigorous redistribution efforts. He denounced his own president and party head, Guzmán, as an upper-class landowner and transitional figure. Guzmán responded by reminding Peña of the need for pragmatism and give-and-take, as well as the difficulties of democratic rule in a country as volatile as the Dominican Republic.

The infighting within the PRD did not diminish once Salvador Jorge Blanco took the reins of power. Jorge's austerity programs, his support of harsh measures against protesters, and his condoning of corruption further divided the party as the once-respected PRD became the subject of ridicule. As the Dominican Republic approached the 1986 presidential elections, the floodgates of factionalism opened when leftists in the party, led by Peña Gómez, clashed with moderates, led by Jacobo Majluta, Guzmán's vice president. The antagonism between these camps became so heated that Peña Gómez and Majluta formed their own suborganizations or "tendencies" within the PRD. Both were reluctant to leave the party, with its huge organization and reputation, but at the same time they could not find any common ideological or personal ground on which to build a concensus.

In 1990, the PRD did field Peña Gómez as its presidential candidate, with Majluta running a poor fourth at the head of his own personalist organization. Peña Gómez finished surprisingly well in the election, considering the infighting that occurred in the PRD convention and the acrimony between the two camps. Yet, for a party that had been the primary voice of the masses for decades and the only party that functioned in a modern capacity, the PRD had fallen into disrepute and disorganization.

As to the future, many in the Dominican Republic expect Peña Gómez to seek the nomination in 1994, although his Haitian background may continue to haunt him at the polls. Much depends on the strength of Bosch and the PLD and the popularity of Balaguer, but the activists within the PRD are anxious to settle their factional disputes and return to the position of prominence within the Dominican party system.

The struggle between the "family of order" and the "family of change" is probably the major arena of Dominican politics, but there are other political actors as well. The Democratic Quisqueyan Party (PQD), the personal apparatus of the former general Elías Wessin y Wessin (who led the conservative forces in the 1965 civil war), has participated without interruption in the modern democratic period, although the base of the PQD is weak and appears to be dwindling.

The most vocal and active of the smaller groups is the Dominican Communist Party (PCD). Led by Narcisio Isa Conde, this party was declared legal during the Guzmán administration. It has a small cadre of student leaders and young professionals but has not attracted much popular support. It criticizes the government for the slowness of its reforms, but its visibility in the form of wall posters and painted slogans is considerably greater than its actual strength.

The catalog of political parties could go on with mention of a number of purely personalistic and small splinter groups that usually surface around election time and disappear shortly thereafter. These parties add color and complexity to the political scene, but their influence is weak and their staying power negligible.

Overall, it is hard to say that a strong and well-institutionalized political party system has been established in the Dominican Republic. The Partido Reformista is likely to split up once Balaguer passes out of politics, but we have seen that conservative and business groups have other means of making their influences felt. With the exception of the Social Christians and the Communists, the minor parties have not been prone to last. Only on the Left, in the PRD, is there a strong and viable political party, and even that has been torn by divisiveness.

THE DECISIONMAKING PROCESS

In most Western democratic systems, the structures of government and the procedures for formulating and implementing public policies are understood to be at the center of national politics. Policy decisions made in this context emerge as a result of complex and often cumbersome bargaining among elected politicians, appointed bureaucrats, strong interest groups, and an articulated public opinion. The slow and difficult process by which policy is determined in such systems is viewed as a necessary evil inherent in the participatory process, the constitutionally defined procedures, and the cautious, incremental approach of democratic decisionmaking.

The Dominican structure and process of decisionmaking has not, historically, always conformed to this Western and democratic tradition. Rather, it combines a great deal of elaborate form with some questionable substance. The Dominican constitutional tradition has long reflected the forms of the U.S. Constitution. In the heyday of Dominican caudilloism, one could always find lavishly detailed constitutions, long lists of human rights, the tripartite separation of powers, festive presidential elections, and power formally defined as emanating from the bottom up. These forms were obviously quite different from the operating realities.

Even in modern times, this gap between constitutional formalities and the actual substance of politics persists. The formal separation of powers barely disguises an imperial presidency, local government is weak or nonexistent, and elections may be rigged or used to ratify a president already in power, rather than provide for genuine choice. Instead of reflecting a diversity of independent institutions and interests involved in an open and competitive policy process, Dominican decisionmaking often remains a closed system in which the president and a handful of cronies can determine policies, without much consultation and with little respect for public opinion or democratic procedures.

The present-day Dominican political system is still modeled closely after that of the United States. A constitution promulgated in 1966 by the Balaguer government provides its legal basis. The constitution establishes the familiar three-part division of powers and a bicameral legislature (a senate of 30 members and a chamber of deputies of 120). The country is organized into twenty-nine provinces, plus the National District (Santo Domingo). Executive power is vested in a president elected by popular vote every four years, assisted by a vice president who runs on the same ticket but has few if any established responsibilities. Neither the president nor the vice president may have engaged in active military or police service for at least a year prior to election. The Dominican constitution also provides for a cabinet appointed by the president, consisting of 12 secretaries of state along with other ministers without portfolio. Finally, the Dominican Republic has a detailed bill of rights in the constitution that mirrors that of the United States.

There are many similarities, at the formal level, between the Dominican and U.S. constitutions. But the underlying political realities are often quite distinct. During Balaguer's rule, the presidency has become the overwhelmingly dominant institution, reversing a trend toward greater legislative assertiveness. The legislative and judicial branches are now decidedly subordinate to the executive branch. The judiciary, in particular, has been in conflict with the executive over issues of salary, independence, and patronage. Balaguer counts on a coalition of loyal government bureaucrats, PRSC officials, military and police enforcers, political cronies, and provincial governors to advise him on policy and carry out his decrees. Although Balaguer does consult with certain cabinet secretaries (namely, the secretary of state for the presidency, along with the minister of finance and the president of the Central Bank), the number of decisionmakers in the Dominican government is quite small and, of course, they are deferential to the wishes of Joaquín Balaguer.

The pattern of systematic constitutional neglect fostered by Balaguer and many of his predecessors does not lie easily. The habits of executive predominance regardless of what the constitution says, of systematic and purposeful violations of human rights, and of illegal military and police activities are deeply ingrained in the Dominican political culture. Yet the Guzmán administration inaugurated in 1978 brought some notable changes to the way the system works.

Guzmán, like Balaguer and perhaps like all Dominican presidents, governed in a highly imperious and personal fashion, at times with little concern for the other branches of government. Guzmán also relied on a small coterie of friends and advisers in the formulation of policy. The differences can be found, however, in the increasing importance of and attention to legislative debate, the institution of a government of laws, respect for human rights, and a tolerance of diversity, even though those who benefited from this tolerance often attacked the government itself.

Perhaps the best illustration of this commitment to constitutionality and democratic government is in the area of human rights. A study done by the U.S. Congress and supported by independent reports from Amnesty International provides ample evidence for the changes ushered in by the Guzmán administration. In 1978, the new government released 200 political prisoners and brought some needed reforms to the infamous prison La Victoria. The government also enacted a liberal amnesty law enabling scores of exiles to return home. These changes, plus greater opportunities for opposition groups to organize, demonstrate, and disseminate literature, earned the Guzmán administration high marks. The Dominican Republic was among the freest and most democratic countries in Latin America.

The changes in the policymaking process and in the functioning of the entire governmental system under Guzmán brought new life and hope to the Dominican Republic. A new sense of national pride became evident. The country ranked right up there with Costa Rica and Venezuela on the major indexes of democracy and human rights. It provided a model of how to shift from authoritarian to democratic rule.

Since retaking the presidency in 1986, Balaguer's record on human rights has been positive. There are certainly incidents of police brutality against urban protesters and accusations that the government intimidates the press and exerts too much control on the media. But unlike the 1970s, when Balaguer seemed helpless (really unwilling) to rein in the paramilitary groups who preyed on opponents of the government, the current Dominican leadership has come to recognize that if tourist and investment dollars are to continue entering the country, it must perpetuate the image of a nation that, at least in the area of human rights, is a democracy in actual practice and not just in form. According to human rights organizations such as Amnesty International, the Dominican Republic has a respectable human rights record, but the ongoing controversy over the treatment of Haitian cane-cutters has tarnished the improvements made during this latest period of democratic rule.[7]

But we must step back from this talk of transformation of the Dominican political system, whether in the area of enhanced legislative power, more aggressive judicial participation, or an extremely human rights record. We must recognize that the processes of social, economic, and political development have been and will continue to be long, arduous, and erratic. There are no quick fixes, no easy solutions. Although Guzmán and the PRD moved to inculcate the spirit of democracy, to foster healthy political discussion and diversity, and to reestablish the rule of law, it must be remembered that these changes were new and not completely institutionalized. In all of Dominican history, after all, there have been only eight or ten years of democratic government, and the interim between the last attempt and Guzmán's was fully fifteen years. Democratic rule is not a system of governance with which the Dominicans have had long experience. Caution is therefore essential when analyzing the current state and future directions of Dominican politics.

Now that Balaguer is in the presidency and has embraced some of the reforms introduced by Guzmán, one can be encouraged that sustained democratic development has arrived in the Dominican Republic. Balaguer has apparently come to realize not only that he must operate in a more open and competitive political environment but also that the use of force or the wanton neglect of constitutionalism has a serious impact on the nation's image. What Balaguer has done as a result is agree to participate in the new democratic environment, while retaining his centralized mode of decisionmaking.

In the Dominican Republic of Joaquín Balaguer, there is still much form and precious little substance in the way democratic government is conducted. Election commissions are formed, legislatures are sometimes consulted, the judiciary is promised a major overhaul and new responsibilities, and the government touts its human rights record. Yet, in reality, elections remain engulfed in fraud, the legislature merely reacts to government initiatives, the judiciary continues to wait for change, and incidents of police and military brutality are announced in the press with disturbing regularity. If there is a lesson to be learned concerning democratic development in the Dominican Republic, it is that though the process of democratic development can be sustained despite economic downturns, the character of political leadership can shape the democracy in ways that limit its effectiveness. Balaguer's legacy may be that he continued to democratize the Dominican Republic—but only on his own terms.

8

Public Policy and Policymaking

Politics in the Dominican Republic is often defined in one-dimensional terms as an unrelenting quest for power and the privileges that accrue from it or as an effort by those who have power and privileges to hang on to them at all costs and by those who don't use whatever means are available to gain some for themselves. That is not an entirely inaccurate portrayal of Dominican politics—at least historically and to a large extent even presently. Dominican politics have become considerably more complex than the sheer struggle for power.

Once in office, political leaders must now face a wide range of problems and public policy issues that require them to make policy decisions on the allocation of scarce resources, the administration of government programs, and the proper direction of national development efforts. Dominican administrations must now rule not just for themselves but also to satisfy popular demands for jobs, housing, water, education, economic development, and social programs of all sorts.

The attention given the problem of power and who controls it has obscured the growing importance of public policy in the Dominican Republic. In the modern era, particularly since Trujillo's death, Dominican politics have matured into a more complex process involving not just a struggle for power but also the provision of government services in a wide range of areas. In short, public policy formulation and implementation has joined (but not superseded) the quest for power and privilege as an essential aspect of Dominican politics.

THE PUBLIC POLICY ENVIRONMENT

The formulation, enactment, and administration of public policy in the Dominican Republic, as elsewhere, is influenced by a unique configuration of social, political, and economic circumstances. In the Dominican

113

Republic, the circumstances in which public policy programs are carried out are well known: widespread poverty, economic dependency, vast social and economic gaps between the several classes, political instability and uncertainty, and intense—and rising—pressures for changes. Together, these and other factors have created formidable barriers to the effective development of public policy programs.

In this policy context, Dominican leaders have been forced to manage and manipulate a variety of domestic and foreign pressures when setting national priorities. A diversity of social and interest groups, economic forces, family alliances, and political party pressures must be satisfied if a policy is to succeed. Frequently, the enactment of a policy must be accompanied by payoffs, patronage, and other favors to disgruntled groups, and individuals. Policy programs that serve a genuinely *public* interest are often lost in the effort to satisfy these private demands. And, of course, in a zero-sum society like the Dominican Republic, if one group gains from such policy measures, another is bound to lose and start plotting against the government.

In this as in other areas, the president remains the focus of the system. He still makes most major public policy decisions and must orchestrate the process of policy implementation. But by this time in the Dominican Republic, there has also developed a large bureaucratic-administrative system. This includes the ministries and a whole range of special agencies and offices for the management of various national programs: energy, water resources, economic development, and others. In addition, the Dominican Republic has a comparatively large industrial sector that is government-owned, consisting chiefly of the former Trujillo businesses that were "inherited" by the government after the Trujillo family fled the country. Hence, while the Dominican public policy process remains president-centered, it has also become a much larger, more complex, and bureaucratized system with all the possibilities for graft, mismanagement, and ineffectiveness that that implies.

AGRICULTURAL VERSUS INDUSTRIAL DEVELOPMENT

One of the most fundamental arguments in the Dominican Republic is whether to assign priority to agricultural or to industrial development. It remains largely a rural, agricultural society with age-old traditions of working the land and the characteristic two-class social patterns of an agrarian society. Industrialization began under Trujillo, and its acceleration in recent decades, coupled with declining prices over a long term for commodities like sugar, have called into question the advisability of relying too heavily on agriculture. Primarily because of the price fluctuations for agricultural commodities, Dominican leaders have become convinced that diversification of the economy is essential for continued, stable growth.[1]

In the post–civil war period, the move toward diversification and industrialization began in earnest. The government moved forward with programs to lure foreign investment, build light industrial centers, explore for minerals, and shift public resources to heavy construction, transportation, and communications. During Balaguer's presidency, new port facilities were built, new leather and garment industries were established, and a variety of other factories began functioning. When Balaguer did shift his attention from industrialization to agriculture, it was usually in the form of grandiose dam building and irrigation projects that benefited large landowners and left small farmers without sorely needed farm machinery, fertilizer, or more modern farming techniques.

The emphasis on industrial development under Balaguer undoubtedly sped up modernization, but it also created numerous social and economic problems that are still being felt today. One by-product was the massive influx of peasants into the cities because agriculture was languishing and there were no incentives to keep small farmers on the land. Massive urban migration has not only contributed further to the decline of agriculture, it has also created immense housing, sanitation, water, electricity, and other shortages in the cities. The daily arrival of hundreds of new city-dwellers has also placed added pressures on an already strained employment market.

Perhaps the most serious problem of the emphasis on industrialization was the failure of agricultural production to keep pace with domestic demand. The country was obliged to import such basic foodstuffs as rice and beans. This revealed the neglect and decline of the agricultural sector, and it forced the government to use scarce financial reserves to feed its own people.

The Guzmán administration came into office with a quite different attitude. Perhaps because of his own farming background or his ideological sympathy for the plight of the peasant, Guzmán sought to redress the imbalance between agricultural and industrial development. He designated 1980 as the "year of agriculture" and moved forward on a number of fronts to rejuvenate the agricultural sector.

Primary emphasis was placed on irrigation, to benefit small farmers as well as large. Although Balaguer had begun some large irrigation projects, he had not provided the complementary facilities to make mechanized watering systems available. Using funds from the IADB, Guzmán sought to provide these facilities for rural irrigation.

Guzmán also expanded the program of rural credit. Coordinating such agencies as the Agricultural Bank, the Institute for Cooperative Development and Credit (IDECOOP), and the Office of Community

Development (ODC), government officials began to provide more financing for small farmers.

The third facet of the government's agricultural policy was price stabilization. The Price Stabilization Institute (INESPRE), formed by Balaguer, is charged with using government funds to purchase domestic agricultural products and thereby ensure growers of a ready market at stable prices. In 1979, under Guzmán, INESPRE invested $10 million in direct purchases from producers. It also entered the foreign importation market to purchase agricultural products. Such importation arrangements, which amounted to $63 million in 1979, are designed to supplement domestic agricultural production in a way that does not jeopardize internal production or depress the fragile pricing mechanism.

The most controversial aspect of agricultural policy is land resettlement. The Guzmán administration pledged a more vigorous program to provide landless peasants with clear titles. In 1979, the government resettled close to a thousand families and distributed to them 137,809 *tareas* (21,500 acres) of land. The government is proud of these agrarian reform efforts, but leftist critics view them as insufficient. The agrarian reform involved the doling out of land already in state hands, not nationalizations. Guzmán took a strong stand against the forcible seizure of private lands by peasants; on a number of occasions, he reminded peasants, who constitute a major part of the government's base of support, that such seizures were illegal and would be met with swift judicial action.

The resettlement program faced major problems. The Dominican Agrarian Institute (IAD), which manages the program, underwent a number of leadership shake-ups and was a focal point of criticism from the government's own party leaders. The PRD leaders were disenchanted with what they feel was an unfulfilled pledge by Guzmán to carry out extensive agrarian reform.

With the election of Salvador Jorge Blanco in 1982, the public policy emphasis shifted to the cities, in large part because the austerity programs and IMF restructuring initiatives sparked urban violence that forced the government to address the needs of those in the barrios of Santo Domingo, rather than the tiny hamlets in the rural areas. Unlike Guzmán, who was a gentleman farmer, Jorge was an urban lawyer who did not share his predecessor's affinity for the land. Although Jorge stressed the importance of expanding agricultural production and providing farmers with support services, the downturn in the economy brought on by falling prices for sugar and ferronickel put a halt to these efforts. By the end of his term, Jorge faced angry farmers calling for higher wages, better prices for their goods, and increased access to credit.

It was during Jorge's administration that the Dominican Republic was also wracked by a scandal over the hiring of Haitians to cut sugarcane.

International human rights organizations accused the Jorge government of engaging in near slave-like policies when it contracted for the services of the Haitian workers. Tensions heated up in the rural areas as racial animosities increased over the unwillingness of the Haitians to return across the border after the cutting season was over. Whiter Dominicans rely on the Haitians to perform tasks that they consider beneath them, and they tend to see their darker-skinned neighbors as inferior. The growth in the number of Haitian immigrants in the Dominican rural areas has ushered in a new era of racial antagonism and violence that requires constant vigilance by local police.[2]

With the end of PRD dominance of the presidency and the rise to power of Joaquín Balaguer, many in the rural areas and advocates of strong agricultural policies were encouraged. Over the years, Balaguer had developed close ties to the rural farmers and had benefited from their political support. His penchant for paternalism played well in the rural areas as the president regularly traveled to the tiny hamlets to hand out land deeds or dedicate new infrastructure projects. Once in office, however, Balaguer faced growing opposition from the rural sector. Government price controls on staple products such as poultry, rice, sugar, and milk led to shortages as farmers refused to produce commodities without the traditional economic supports. A scarcity of investment capital in agriculture also angered farmers who were anxious to modernize their operations. Finally, the roller-coaster effect of U.S. sugar quotas brought uncertainty and unemployment to the largest rural employer and placed greater pressure on the government to diversify agriculture in order to incorporate nontraditional products and attract foreign agribusiness investment.

The renewed emphasis by Guzmán on agriculture did not shake what is now a continuing commitment to industrialization and diversification. New manufacturing plants continue to be encouraged and the desire to entice further foreign investment in the industrial sector remains, although with a firmer resolve to achieve more favorable contractual arrangements for the nation.

Where Guzmán placed emphasis on agriculture, Jorge and Balaguer clearly believed the future of the Dominican Republic lay in manufacturing. Manufacturing now accounts for 16 percent of the gross domestic product and has a dollar value of $7.2 billion. Furthermore, much government effort has been directed toward ensuring this sector's continued growth. The government has formed a number of agencies designed to assist in financing, developing, and staffing new industrial enterprises. The Investment Fund for Economic Development (FIDE) pools financial resources from various public, private, and international institutions and acts as a credit agency offering long-term repayment schedules and low interest rates for new industrial concerns. The Industrial Development

Corporation (CFI) is another government agency that acts as a financing agent assisting industries that seek to meet domestic consumer needs. The Dominican Institute of Industrial Technology (INDOTEC) has been established for (among other responsibilities) training workers in the skills necessary for an expanding industrial sector.

The prospect for greater industrial growth in the Dominican Republic in the 1990s seems promising. After some years of little growth in the 1980s, manufacturing made modest gains as the country entered a new decade. With extensive support and financing, from the government and continued interest from foreign investors, both because of the incentives and the low labor costs, manufacturing will likely continue to expand. Moreover, the continued development of the free zones, coupled with enhanced trade possibilities in the United States and Europe, can only heighten the likelihood of a sustained period of industrial expansion. Nevertheless, debate will probably continue over the proper balance between agricultural and industrial development. With the Dominican Republic forced to import basic foodstuffs, thereby intensifying its debt problem, the argument is made within Dominican policy circles that renewed attention needs to be placed on agriculture. In the next few years, it is likely that Dominican policymakers will give added attention to the issues of agricultural credit and rural infrastructure, as well as the controversial topic of price supports in an increasingly privatized economy. It is issues such as these that may galvanize the rural sectors and force the government to face the fact that its push for industrialization has brought promise to some and disappointment to others.

THE PLACE OF SOCIAL WELFARE PROGRAMS IN A MODERNIZING ECONOMY

Even more serious than the dispute between agricultural and industrial policy priorities has been the debate over social welfare programs. At the core of the dispute is the reality of a poor country with limited resources and tight budgetary restrictions, as opposed to the rising public demand for greater spending on health care, housing, social security, and other essential human services.

The dilemma of allocating scarce government resources in a way that responds effectively to the social wants and needs of the population is one that will not be easily resolved. The Dominican government can put its limited capital into investments for the future or it can spend it on social programs that satisfy immediate needs, but it cannot do both. Hence, social welfare policy has become the most hotly contested issue in Dominican politics today. Starting with the 1978 presidential campaign, Dominican political leaders have been debating the proper balance of domestic priorities: investment versus consumption; infrastructure needs versus human needs. The Balaguer legacy from 1966–1978 was one of a builder and modernizer whose budget figures during his years in office showed a clear preference for spending for the armed forces and capital construction, together with some noticeable increases for education.

Guzmán and the PRD, in contrast, promised less attention to construction and infrastructure development and more to social programs. But in office, Guzmán found that such a reordering of spending priorities was not so easy. Key social and economic elites questioned the need for expanded social programs and argued both that the country could not afford them and that longer-term economic development would have to be sacrificed.

An early dispute occurred over housing, a Guzmán priority. The president of the nation's Central Bank, a Balaguer supporter, blocked a government housing credit of $32 million on the grounds it was inflationary. The decision by the bank drew howls of protest from the PRD. Guzmán's own economic coordinator lashed out at the bank's decision as a failure to respond to legitimate social demands. Guzmán was caught in the middle. As the leader of the PRD, he sympathized with the frustration of fellow party members eager to carry out a key part of the party program. But as president, he recognized the necessity of maintaining balance, holding down inflation, and continuing to work amicably with powerful economic officials and institutions. In the end, he fired his PRD adviser and bore the brunt of the party's criticism; the housing program was blocked.

The problems faced by Guzmán in shifting Dominican public policy priorities toward social welfare were magnified under the administration of Jorge Blanco, who had to endure four years of relentless economic decline and disorder that severely limited his ability to address pressing domestic needs. Jorge found himself dismantling programs and delaying implementation of benefits as he labored to deal with IMF restructuring guidelines and citizen protests over a declining quality of life. It was during the Jorge administration that Dominicans came to realize that the miracle was, indeed, over and that the government could no longer provide the kind of safety net that was beginning to be established during the years in which the economy was strong.[3]

The victory of Joaquín Balaguer in 1986 brought hope to many Dominicans who felt that the aged leader would restore the economy and renew the benefits, albeit meager, that the government had provided. Balaguer responded to the need to address the crisis in the domestic scene by his vaunted public construction program. Rather than begin new social welfare programs or expand existing ones, he chose jobs creation and infrastructure development as the key ingredients to enhance the lives of the average Dominican.[4] For a time, this tactic worked, with new housing construction not only meeting a basic need of the growing population but also addressing one of the perennial economic problems in the country— unemployment. If one defines social welfare in a broader context to include those services provided by the government, beyond safety net programs for the poor, that contribute to the quality of life, then the Balaguer government did deal with one facet of social welfare, but at the expense of many others. By the 1990 election, this government was being roundly criticized for ignoring some of the basic needs of the people, including potable water, electricity, and clean streets.

The lesson of social welfare policy under the Guzmán, Jorge, and Balaguer administrations is that government actions to reorder national priorities in a situation of scarce resources cannot be separated from the realities of economic and political power. Whereas modernization in the industrial and agricultural sectors is something on which virtually all groups can agree (although obviously differing on priorities) and from which all can benefit, social welfare programs imply choices concerning which groups and classes will receive the major benefits from government programs. Social programs are designed primarily for the poor, who are the largest group numerically but are politically (so far) the weakest in the country. They thus run up against the opposition of the economic elites who have other priorities and the political influence to back up their preferences. They also confront the changing economic climate and the policy preferences of political leaders. From 1978 through 1991, three Dominican presidents made social welfare policy at a time of widespread recession and dislocation. Not surprisingly, their responses to social welfare needs during the economic crisis were different, as Guzmán sought unsuccessfully to reorder priorities, Jorge was forced to delay action on many of his priorities, and Balaguer engaged in stopgap measures that addressed some priorities while leaving others unattended.

Agricultural and industrial policy are important in terms of the country's long-range development, but social programs are also necessary both to relieve human suffering and to test a democratic government's capacity to achieve justice and a more equitable division of wealth and power. The balance is not easy to strike, as is shown by the efforts of the last three presidents to improve the quality of life amidst a declining economy and an ever-restive population.

AUSTERITY AND THE QUALITY OF ECONOMIC GROWTH

Decisions on priorities and budget allocations in poor countries like the Dominican Republic are difficult. Most of them do not involve simple choices between moral good and evil but choices between lesser evils. This is also true with the debate over austerity.

Austerity implies the putting off of benefits and consumption now for the sake of promised benefits in some distant and usually vague future. The burden of austerity generally falls on the shoulders of the poor. In the Dominican Republic, austerity measures have been used to restrict current consumption in order to generate greater capital for investment or other purposes. From 1966 to 1978, Balaguer used a variety of austerity measures to control inflation and make available the necessary revenue for his development programs. For example, most strikes were declared illegal, as a way of helping hold down wages. Food prices were allowed to rise as a means of cutting consumption. State workers were refused pay increases for the entire twelve years of Balaguer's rule. Only in 1979, under Guzmán, did the state workers finally get a pay raise along with a new law providing for a minimum wage of $125 a month, paid vacation time, and a guaranteed Christmas bonus.

Balaguer's austerity programs affected not just workers but the aged, the poor, and the disabled as well. Pensions during Balaguer's presidency remained at $30 per month, even in the face of inflation at nearly 20 percent during some of those years. Programs for the disabled were also cut back. The Guzmán administration sought to improve conditions in the homes for the disabled and raised pensions to $100 a month, a great improvement over the previous figure but still paltry as a sum to try to live on.

Balaguer followed an intensive austerity program, but Guzmán had to continue many of the same or similar policies. The decision by the government to raise gasoline prices from $1.25 to $1.85 per gallon in 1979 may have been necessary to reduce consumption and pay for foreign oil, but it was also a devastating blow to urban workers, jitney drivers, and truckers whose work requires cheap and available fuel. Guzmán's image as a man of the people was severely damaged as a result of the price hike decision, which also helped to reinforce the view of the Left that Guzmán was a conservative oligarch in PRD clothing.

The controversy over the use of stringent austerity measures came to a head during the administration of President Jorge Blanco. By 1982, the Dominican Republic was drifting deeper and deeper into the morass of debt, trade imbalance, negative growth, and insolvency. To ease the serious balance of payments crisis, Jorge increased prices on basic foods and oil products anywhere from 50 to 200 percent in 1984. The drastic pricing measures were joined by other decisions to limit imports and devalue the peso, all with the intent of complying with IMF guidelines and attracting more U.S. assistance.[5]

The process of imposing austerity measures, which had been followed by urban unrest, started again in 1985 when the Jorge government raised the price of gasoline and devalued the peso. The threat of a national strike and the realization that the PRD government was losing its natural constituency among the masses forced Jorge to rescind some of the increases and agree to raise minimum wages and government salaries. The government was clearly buying time with the wage and price policies in the hope that the export of Dominican goods would improve and that further assistance from the United States and commercial banks would be forthcoming. Although Jorge finished his term in 1986 without further uprisings, his decision to introduce austerity policies that limited the purchasing power of the Dominican people revived many of the class antagonisms and political frustrations that had been suppressed by Balaguer and put aside during the democratic euphoria of the Guzmán years.

Once Balaguer reentered the presidency, he initially moved away from austerity measures and dependence on IMF funding and guidelines. But as the Dominican economy continued to falter, he was also forced to deny wage increases, cut public budgets, and lay off bureaucrats. In addition, ever-rising oil costs, coupled with shortages brought on by the Persian Gulf War, led to new protests as the government sought to deal with the realities of dependency. Although Balaguer was more savvy in handling his austerity program and gained some support because of his nationalistic position on negotiating with the IMF, he was eventually required to follow in Jorge's footsteps by limiting imports, devaluing the peso, increasing prices, and strengthening tax collections.

In contemporary Dominican politics, there has been little room for presidents to maneuver around the need for austerity measures. Politicians such as Jorge and Balaguer may try to delay the impact of austerity or lessen the financial burden by piecemeal allocation of the costs, but in the end, the government cannot avoid the need to develop policies that restructure the economy and the monetary system, especially because foreign governments and multilateral lending institutions require compliance in return for loans and credits.

FOUR POLICIES: POPULATION, ENERGY, EDUCATION, AND TAXATION

We have looked at agricultural policy, industrial policy, and welfare policy. It can be argued that success in these areas is dependent on success in other socioeconomic policy areas, most notably family planning, energy policy, educational policy, and taxation. Indeed, posing the issue in this way serves to show how interrelated the vicious circles of Dominican underdevelopment are and how intractable the problems are.

Population Policy

The Dominican Republic has long seen its population problems in terms of too small a population rather than too great a population. Emptied and depopulated during the colonial era, devastated still further during the Haitian occupation, and fearful subsequently that Haiti, with its greater numbers but smaller territory, would overwhelm the whole island, the policy of virtually all Dominican governments has been to seek to increase the population through immigration and incentives for large families.

Family planning did not emerge as a major issue until the 1960s. The first family planning efforts were carried out by private individuals, then the government made some weak and tentative efforts to encourage family planning, and finally, in 1968, the Balaguer government created a National Council on Population and the Family to oversee an official family planning program. Funds and planning for the program come almost exclusively from the United States.

The program has been controversial for a long time. The church was opposed but was persuaded to maintain a low profile. The Left was opposed. So was the Right, which wanted to maintain a strong barrier against Haiti's possible intrusions and also wished to keep a large, cheap labor supply. In addition, many poor Dominicans saw large numbers of children as a means to increase family income by putting more hands in the field and as a form of social security insurance in old age.

But the government was persuaded that its ambitious programs in housing, education, economic development, and other areas would be in vain unless population growth was checked. The government has since opened several hundred clinics, approved a considerable publicity campaign focused on maternal/child health, and sent some 2,000 community health workers to go door-to-door, especially in poor and rural areas, to talk about health, nutrition, and family planning matters.

Since the 1960s, the population growth rate has fallen from about 3.5 percent per year to about 2.4 percent today. Meanwhile, the Dominican Republic has achieved population parity with Haiti, there are no more open spaces in the country suitable for homesteading, and basic services (water, electricity, refuse) in the country's major cities, especially Santo Domingo, are breaking down because of overcrowding. Now, everyone agrees that the Dominican Republic has a population problem.

The government's policies have been responsible for some of the decline in population growth rates. But of ever-greater importance has been emigration, chiefly to Puerto Rico and the United States, as well as such "natural" causes as education and urbanization because "more hands" makes less sense in the cities than in the countryside. Family planning programs are well established, but the results in terms of actually reaching women of childbearing age or of significantly affecting the population growth rate are still quite meager. Because the Dominican Republic's population problem for the next two generations involves people who have already been born, the pressures on the land, social services, and the political system continue to build.

The character of Dominican emigration has also changed over this same time frame. In the past, the emigration of Dominicans was a mere trickle compared to what it is now, and most of those who left tended to return. Now, the trickle has become a flood, whole families are leaving instead of just the men, and the exodus is often permanent. The Dominican colony in New York City has grown to several hundred thousand persons, and from this enclave, Dominican colonies have spread to other areas of the United States. It seems that almost all Dominican families have relatives, friends, or neighbors who live in the United States, and there is a considerable flow of family members back and forth. The whole sociology of the Dominican family has been greatly affected by the emigration patterns.[6]

Energy Development

Much has been said about Dominican dependency and its effects on the country's internal economic situation. Although the dependency issue is often discussed in terms of trade and investments, perhaps the most critical area of Dominican dependence is its heavy reliance on foreign oil. Present energy imports exceed export revenues by $100 million yearly. The Dominicans are acutely conscious of this imbalance and are making adjustments, especially in tourism and manufacturing, as a way of increasing earnings to pay the rising oil bill. Nevertheless, the domestic demand for oil has not abated, as population pressures and a more diversified economy create ever-greater need.

To meet the energy crisis, the Guzmán administration formed a special National Commission for Energy Policy, whose mission was to find "ways to reduce reliance on oil imports and to identify sectors where significant conservation can be achieved." To meet this objective, the government, through its energy agency, the Dominican Electric Power Corporation (CDE), began extensive oil exploration (conducted jointly with U.S. firms), research into the feasibility of using bagasse (the husks of sugarcane) as an energy source, and serious examination of solar energy, which many feel has a real future in that sun-drenched country.

Because this search for alternative energy sources is largely future-oriented, recent governments have been involved in finding short-run answers to meet the country's more immediate needs. Early in 1980, Guzmán announced the commitment of $142 million for improvements

Valdesia dam (*Warren Smith; courtesy of Public Affairs Analysts, Inc.*)

in existing power systems and an agreement with Spain for planning studies on the proposed Higuey–El Aguacate dam, which would provide an additional 200 megawatts of power to meet the country's expanding needs.

The Dominican-Spanish agreement is part of a larger pattern of energy development in the Dominican Republic that seeks to have the country's energy needs filled by tapping the scores of rivers that flow from the major mountain ranges. The development of hydroelectric power, Dominicans feel, enables them to harness energy from these rivers and also aids the agricultural sector by channeling water to areas in need of irrigation. Such projects also help serve the water needs of the capital. The Madrigal Dam provides an additional 50,000 kilowatts of power to Santo Domingo and should also give its residents sufficient potable water until the year 2000.

The construction of hydroelectric dams has been one of the primary areas of international financial assistance to the Dominican Republic.

Besides the long-standing interest of Spain in these projects, the government has also received assistance from the IADB, the World Bank, the United States Export-Import Bank, and other foreign commercial banks. Such outlays of foreign assistance have been used by the government to develop twenty-eight hydroelectric plants, with more planned for the future.

Yet, despite these broad-based efforts to conserve and develop energy, the Dominican Republic has been burdened in recent years by a failure to meet the growing electrical needs of its population and its newly expanded industrial base. The Balaguer years from 1986 to the present have been marked by regular brownouts, as outdated and overworked generators have failed to provide continuous service. In 1989, unpredictable power outages occurred, on average, about five hours per day. Although the Dominican Electric Corporation, a state enterprise, has a generating capacity of 1,100 megawatts, it provides only between 400 and 500 megawatts and sometimes even less when equipment is out of service. International aid consultants estimated that transmission losses and theft of electricity account for over 30 percent of power output.

In the view of many Dominican analysts, the brownouts were the major catalyst in the opposition to Balaguer in 1990 for Dominicans appeared disgusted with the inability of the government to deal with the electrical problem. Sensing the growing animosity toward his government over the energy issue, Balaguer began a major program to attract foreign energy development and support, make the CDE a more efficient bureaucracy, and gradually introduce privatization initiatives that would transform the CDE into a market-driven enterprise. To date, Balaguer has been partially successful in achieving his objectives. He negotiated a $105-million project with the World Bank to improve generation, along with a series of bilateral arrangements with foreign governments and commercial businesses to modernize existing equipment. In 1990, the government began downsizing the CDE, which, together with the state sugar company, contributed $104 million to the 1989 public sector deficit. Balaguer cut the staff of the CDE by 40 percent and imposed surcharges on electric bills. In the area of privatization, Balaguer has dragged his feet, in large part because there is great opposition to the dismantling of the public sector with its job creation and patronage possibilities. Balaguer did, however, sign a law in 1990 allowing for and encouraging private generation, transmission, and sale of electricity, although the law is not as sweeping as many in the business community had hoped.[7]

By 1991, the efforts of the government were beginning to bear some fruit: The regularity of the brownouts and the complaining decreased. Also, most foreign industries in the Dominican Republic, as well as hotels, import their own generators and produce their own electricity, which has become an accepted way of doing business in the country. Nevertheless, the nation's long-term energy picture is still bleak. Dependence on foreign oil, heightened demand, outdated equipment, and a continuing contraction in growth (an 8.3 percent contraction in 1989) indicate that energy is one public policy area that will remain at the forefront of political debate into the next century.

Educational Expansion

In the less developed world, education is correctly viewed as an essential ingredient of development and a means of drawing people out of poverty. In the Dominican Republic, recent administrations have recognized the importance of education as an "engine" of progress and change, but they have been unable to provide the necessary resources to use education to transform the economy and the country. After the key election in 1978, President Guzmán initiated a number of educational reforms. He called for the complete overhaul of the middle (roughly, junior high) school and for greater adult education programs in the country. The administration seemed most concerned about the continued high rate of illiteracy, a staggering dropout rate after the first few years of school, and the paucity of vocational programs that are essential if the country is to meet the demands of increased industrialization.

The commitment of the Guzmán administration to education was not mere words. A comparison of the education appropriation for 1978 (Balaguer's last year) and 1979 (Guzmán's first year) points clearly to an expanded emphasis on education.

The Guzmán administration's budgetary increases for education produced quick results. In 1979, 490 new schools with a total of 1,000 classrooms were built at a cost of $16.7 million. Guzmán also began programs to increase opportunities for vocational education and to reduce illiteracy.

But as the Dominican Republic slipped deeper and deeper into trade deficits, foreign indebtedness, and stagflation, the commitment to education became more difficult to sustain. Guzmán's successors, Jorge and Balaguer, were unable to match his modernization programs in education. To a large extent, they only kept pace with population pressures and did little to address the serious education deficiencies of the country. In 1985, for example, 48 percent of Dominicans over twenty-five had no formal schooling, with only 2 percent completing a higher education degree. As Table 8.1 points out, there has been no major upward push recently in education financing, as was evidenced during the first year of the Guzmán administration. The most revealing comparison of the Jorge and Balaguer governments shows that the Jorge allocation for education in 1985 was 12

TABLE 8.1   Educational Appropriations: Guzmán, Jorge, and Balaguer Compared

	Guzmán 1981	Jorge 1985	Balaguer 1989
Total education (RD$ millions)	131.2	253.0	393.0
% for education in total budget	11.9	12.0	6.6

Source: Dominican government.

percent of the total budget, and Balaguer's education allocation for 1989 (the last year for which figures are available) was but 6.6 percent of the total. In the Balaguer years, the public monies were diverted to the office of the presidency and to the military—the former as a means of distributing patronage and infrastructure projects, the latter to ensure political support.

If there has been a bright spot in education during the Jorge and Balaguer years, it has been the greater interest shown in vocational education. Funded by foreign assistance programs and training seminars from free zone investors, Dominicans are acquiring the skills necessary to provide the technical and, in some cases, managerial support to the ever-growing free zone industries. Dominicans continue to be viewed by foreign investors as easily trainable and willing to work toward self-improvement.

To date, the Dominican government has a mixed record on education. Although there has been some improvement in the literacy rate and encouraging changes in vocational education are seen, the high volume of dropouts, the miniscule number of students who attend college, and the inability of the government to properly fund education seriously hampers the prospects for economic development. The hard task of matching education programs with the economic and development needs of the country—rather than simply producing more waifs to shine shoes or sell fruit—is yet to be accomplished.

Tax Policy

In many Latin American countries, the taxation policies of the government have never occupied the center stage of domestic politics. Governments in the region have generally adopted rather loose tax policies, often bowing to pressure from powerful landed and business interests. In the Dominican Republic, tax policies and tax collections are much in line with the overall Latin American experience. Currently, the Dominican government imposes a progressive personal income tax, a corporate tax, and a value-added tax. In addition, the government has developed a wide range of trade tariffs that provide the largest source of government revenue because collection of the income and corporate taxes are regularly evaded or these funds are uncollectible due to weak tax administration.

The income tax is comparable to that found in the United States, although the rates are higher (as much as 70 percent) and there are no deductions. The corporate income tax is progressive and begins at 10 percent for earnings under RD$5,000, rising 49.4 percent of earnings over RD$250,000. Also, dividends and interest payments remitted overseas are subject to a 35 percent withholding tax. In 1983, with amendments added in 1984 and 1989, the Dominican government also instituted a value-added tax of 6 percent, which is extended to all stages of production.

Because tax evasion is pervasive in the Dominican Republic, the government has allocated its enforcement resources to tariff collection. A new tariff program was put into effect in 1990, designed to address the large number of exemptions provided for certain goods and certain import sectors and to provide some general tariff relief. Over the next four years, tariffs on luxury goods will increase substantially, although there will be exemptions for basic food, agricultural inputs, medicine, and power-generating equipment. The government feels that by increasing some tariffs on consumer goods while decreasing other tariffs on staple commodities and equipment related to industry, additional revenue will be raised without jeopardizing foreign investment and economic growth.

Perhaps the most generous tax policy of the Dominican government concerns the free zones and the tourist industry. According to Dominican law, free zones are exempt from tariffs, foreign exchange conversion, and corporate income taxes for twenty years, and tourism projects are exempt from income and corporate taxes for ten years. The Balaguer government, in particular, has sent out a clear signal to the international investment community that tax incentives are being promulgated with the express purpose of attracting foreign capital and technology to the Dominican Republic.[8]

The generally positive tax climate in the Dominican Republic, whether legally constituted or illegally avoided, has created significant business opportunities but also contributed to regular revenue shortfalls. Collecting all the taxes owed the government would not solve the nation's problems, but with tax evasion so prominent in the country, the collection of each citizen's fair share of taxes would certainly allow the government to provide more services, enlarge the safety net, and initiate more infrastructure projects. It is in part because of poor tax collection that the Dominican Republic is forced to rely on foreign borrowing and regular reductions in its public sectors budgets.

PUBLIC POLICY AND THE FUTURE OF
DOMINICAN DEVELOPMENT

The Dominican Republic has modernized a great deal in the last two decades, and the significant progress achieved in various public policy fields bodes well for the future. Yet one must not think of this development as inevitable or unilinear. Setbacks and reversals are always possible, the external environment may upset even the best-conceived plans, and the play of internal political and social forces may yet produce chaos and breakdown.

The Dominican Republic, first and foremost, is a poor, underdeveloped, and dependent nation. It is dependent economically in the sense that it must rely on external markets to sell and buy its goods, and it is dependent politically and militarily as a small nation lying within what the United States considers its sphere of influence. This external dependency affects the country's ability to sustain its developmental efforts. With revenue, investment capital, trade, and technology all dependent on decisions and forces made or located outside its borders, the government must devote at least as much attention to these external pressures as to the internal ones. It is subject to a host of pressures and changes that it has no capacity to control.

As modern Dominican history attests, when the external context is favorable, considerable internal development can also occur. But when such "dependency variables" as declining sugar revenues, increased prices for oil, inflated prices for imported manufactured goods, reduced capital investment, shortages of technical equipment also imported from the outside, or U.S. disfavor of a regime or policy are introduced into the picture, the country may not only experience delays and sometimes severe setbacks in its development efforts, but its fragile political system may be destabilized as well.

The often damaging impact of these dependency variables coupled with uncertain "governing variables," can make Dominican development extremely shaky and uncertain. Deep-seated political divisions, a sometimes interventionist military, ineffective or corrupt administration, and a weak system of representative government have created a public policy environment that is extremely tenuous. The effective implementation of worthwhile public policies cannot be very successfully carried out in a climate of suspicion, distrust, fear, antagonism, and divisionism.

The solution, of course, would be a happy mix of dependency and governing variables, but Dominican public policy in the contemporary era has generally not operated in such a favorable climate. Under Balaguer, the Dominican Republic was led by a man for whom the dependency variables (that is, relations with the outside world, high sugar prices, and so forth) were unusually favorable. Balaguer was able to achieve his economic miracle precisely because these external conditions were so propitious and because the surpluses generated could be used to keep the governing variables in check; in other words, the economic pie was sufficiently large and expanding that many who might otherwise go into opposition could also share the pieces.

Balaguer's miracle eventually turned into a disaster as a result of the reversal of precisely the same factors that had created the original boom. By 1974, sugar prices had plummeted, oil prices skyrocketed, and investment income slackened off. Growth rates that had been in the 9–12 percent range dropped to 4–5 percent. These external economic and dependency forces caused a massive downturn in the economy and, with a smaller pie to cut up, also activated the governing variables, the internal political opposition forces that accelerated the decline of the Balaguer regime. Balaguer, the once-secure builder and modernizer of Dominican society, who had enjoyed widespread support, now faced angry crowds, a restive military, charges of malfeasance, and a renewed political challenge from a worthy opponent.

Guzmán wrestled with these same dependency and governing forces and had to weigh carefully the impact they would have on the prospects for both economic development and political stability. The external dependency variables largely control the overall pace and quality of Dominican modernization, and these, in turn, help shape the internal, more immediate, governing variables and forces, which are capable of overthrowing a government.

Jorge took office at a time in which the dependency forces and the governing forces collided, as the Dominican Republic hovered near economic collapse and social anarchy. The government was forced to rely even more heavily on the external sector as it embraced IMF loans in return for IMF restructuring guidelines. This reliance on external funding and policy guidance fostered intense social and political opposition that erupted in regular urban violence throughout 1984 and 1985. By the end of Jorge's administration, the Dominican Republic had achieved a degree of stability but at the cost of further dependency and the tarnishing of social democracy.

The rise again to power of Joaquín Balaguer in 1986 brought hope to those who felt the aged leader would not be as willing to bow to pressure from the international community and would chart a more independent course. Although Balaguer resisted following the IMF guidelines and did begin the process of creating an economy that had the potential for greater independence, the Dominican Republic opened itself up to a new kind of dependency as it tied its future to the investment decisions of foreign businesses and tourists. Dependence on sugar had been replaced by dependence on investment capital. For a time, this strategy brought a degree of stability, but Balaguer too faced new problems of governance that were unfamiliar to him. Dominicans began to question his judgment and his policy decisions. The centralized and smooth-running policy process began to come apart as a wide spectrum of groups voiced their displeasure over his failure to transform the new dependency into the new prosperity. Like his predecessors, Balaguer had to endure public protest and urban violence, and he eventually began the process of negotiating with the IMF for loans and policy reforms.

It must always be remembered that in the Dominican Republic, the probability of rapid change is extremely high in both the external and the internal conditions, which makes the tenure of any government very uncertain. A clever and prudent president can manage some of these forces through his own initiatives, but if he is realistic, he will also recognize that some of them are entirely out of his hands. That is also true of the Dominican public policy process in general: It is, in large part, subject to forces, external and internal, that are only partially predictable and controllable and that may offer very few clues as to the extent of their impact on either economic or political development.

9

The Dominican Republic in the International Arena

One of the most fascinating aspects of the Dominican Republic is the high level of visibility—whether through its own efforts or as a victim of the actions of other nations—that is has maintained in the international arena throughout its history. Other countries in Latin America with larger populations or land areas have not been at the center stage of world politics as often as the Dominican Republic has. Unfortunately, the worldwide visibility or perhaps notoriety of the Dominican Republic has, in many instances, not been the result of its own initiatives but the result of foreign intervention in its internal affairs, its dependency relations, or its tumultuous internal politics. The Dominican Republic has an international importance all out of proportion to its size, population, or resources.

Because of its location, the nation has historically been of major strategic significance. Hispaniola is the second largest island in the Caribbean. It lies athwart the major trade routes from Europe to the Caribbean and Central America and from the U.S. east coast to the Panama Canal and all of South America. From the sixteenth through the eighteenth centuries, when the Caribbean was one of the world's most important imperial frontiers, all the major powers—Spain, France, England, Holland—sought to conquer Hispaniola. The United States is only the most recent in a long history of great powers that have tried to dominate the island and the Dominican Republic.

DOMINICAN-U.S. RELATIONS

The importance of the Dominican Republic to the United States stems, in large part, from its strategic geographic position in the Caribbean and the long-standing view of the United States that the Caribbean is in *its* sphere of influence and must be protected. The attitude that the Caribbean is an "American backyard" and its southern first line of defense has been held by all U.S. presidents since James Monroe. Uncomfortable in the face, successively, of a French, British, Spanish, German, and most recently Soviet presence so close to its shores, the United States has repeatedly intervened in the internal affairs of its weak Caribbean neighbors. With few reservations and no respect for the sovereignty of the Dominican Republic, U.S. presidents have threatened and cajoled, "negotiated" trade and lending arrangements manifestly unfair to the Dominican Republic, administered and collected Dominican export revenues for the United States, advocated full annexation as a means of guaranteeing domination, and, on two eventual occasions, sent the U.S. Marines to occupy the country and redirect the course of its history.[1]

The Dominican Republic, in many respects, has become a major symbol of Latin American vulnerability to foreign, in particular U.S., domination. Latin Americans see in the Dominican Republic the sad results of proximity to the "colossus of the north." Even though many Latin American countries have experienced foreign intervention or dependent economic relations or have become pawns in world conflict, the Dominican Republic stands most prominently as a nation whose historical unfolding has been a constant reminder of the power of outside forces.

The relationship of the United States to the Dominican Republic can best be described as one of "suprasovereignty." The term "suprasovereignty" is used here because it conveys the idea that the United States not only reacts to internal Dominican events in ways that alter the small nation's politics and development but also makes decisions affecting the Dominican Republic as if *it* (the United States) were sovereign. From the days of Grant's attempted annexation to Roosevelt's customs receivership to Wilson's occupations, Kennedy's interventions, Johnson's sending of the marines, and Carter's human rights policy, the United States has viewed the Dominican Republic not as an independent nation but as a dependency or satellite. The United States has repeatedly sought to place its stamp on the course of Dominican history.

From the perspective of the United States, its suprasovereignty in the Dominican Republic has had a positive impact on Dominican society. As numerous U.S. presidents and policymakers have sought to emphasize, U.S. action also brought, at times, stability, economic growth, and modernization to the Dominicans. Many Dominicans also recognize the advantages of these ties, which helps explain their love-hate attitudes toward the United States. But many are also concluding that in this unequal relationship, the United States has been the major beneficiary, using the Dominican Republic as a pawn in the international power struggle and as a source of needed resources. The Dominicans view the United States as the ultimate arbiter of their destiny and as the prime beneficiary of an unequal "partnership."[2]

In the contemporary period, the foreign policy issues of U.S.-Dominican relations have revolved around anticommunism and, to a lesser extent, the desire to create a model of liberalism and democracy in the Caribbean. With the rise of the cold war and the fear of Soviet expansionism, the United States sought allies in Latin America who would champion the cause of anticommunism. In dictator Rafael Trujillo, the United States found a staunch "anti-Communist" and rewarded him for his loyalty and vigilance with lucrative trade and aid packages and tacit acceptance of his dictatorial regime. In turn, Trujillo posed as "the best friend of the United States in Latin America" and the "foremost anti-Communist in the hemisphere." But when Trujillo overreached himself and it looked like his regime was coming to an end, the United States turned against its longtime ally and sought to pursue its anticommunism in another form.

The United States under John F. Kennedy sought to preserve stability and prevent communism not by aiding dictators but by supporting liberal democrats. It was reasoned that a liberal-democratic reform program was a better defense against communism than a right-wing dictator (the example of Fulgencio Batista in Cuba was in everyone's mind) who would create or perpetuate the conditions under which communism might thrive. In Juan Bosch, the United States thought it had found a democratic alternative to Castroism. Unfortunately for Bosch and liberal democracy, U.S. support was halfhearted and easily overcome. When Bosch angered conservatives by appearing soft on leftists, the United States turned away and allowed its "experiment in democracy" to give way to a military coup.

The anticommunism of the United States was dominated by the "no second Cuba" doctrine. U.S. officials were adamant that "Castro-communism" not be allowed to spread further in Latin America. Hence, when the Dominicans launched their revolution in 1965 to restore constitutional democracy, which U.S. officials thought might produce a Castro-like regime, the United States intervened militarily to prevent the revolution from succeeding.

The defeat of the constitutionalist movement and the manipulation that helped produce Joaquín Balaguer's electoral victory showed the world and particularly the Dominicans the depth of the U.S. fear of communism (or what was thought to be communism) and how far the United States would go to prevent it. To many in the United States, the intervention achieved a double success: A potentially pro-Castro government was prevented from coming to power with minimal losses of American lives and in a relatively short period of time (in contrast to the Vietnam imbroglio), while the new leadership these events produced (Balaguer) was pro-American and presented an image of moderate democracy. Most Dominicans, of course, saw the intervention in quite another light.[3]

During Balaguer's return to "normalcy," 1966–1978, the anti-Communist issue remained largely dormant. There was considerable U.S. assistance in the early years to help the Dominican Republic recover from the devastation of the revolution, but after that, the Dominican Republic was essentially ignored. Relations between the two countries were dominated mainly by economic issues (trade, aid, sugar prices), not by the hotter political controversies of the immediate past. Through its assistance, the United States helped prop up the Balaguer government, and Balaguer was clever at manipulating the United States to gain advantages for himself.

The 1978 election campaign between Balaguer and Guzmán revived the issues of both Castro's Cuba and whether liberal democracy or authoritarianism was the best defense against communism in the Dominican Republic. The foreign policy issue of major concern in the campaign was whether Cuba should be recognized. Some of Guzmán's initial speeches suggested that the country should rethink its earlier break in diplomatic and economic relations with Cuba. But though Guzmán seemed interested in merely exploring the issue, leftists in the PRD, like Peña Gómez, were promoting recognition of Cuba as a major plank in the party's platform.

The Cuba issue was eventually overshadowed by the military's efforts to halt the ballot count and suppress the issue of whether democracy in the Dominican Republic would even survive. With the outcome hanging in the balance, President Carter acted to support Guzmán and his claim of victory. Threatening to cut off aid and strongly supporting the principle of democratic choice, Carter was able to intimidate Balaguer and the military and to guarantee a democratic outcome.

The position taken by Carter seemed a refreshing departure from the past, but one must be careful not to overstate the differences. Dominicans and Latin Americans alike joined in praise of the U.S. action. But in retrospect, it should be noted that the vigorous defense of democracy by Carter was made easier by the absence of any perceived Communist threat at the time. It has always been easy for the United States to support democracy during such noncrisis times; it is in revolutionary and unstable circumstances, when the actors are not so well known and the outcomes more uncertain that the United States is prone to support the other side. And it is likely that, given Balaguer's advanced age and infirmity, the United States perceived Guzmán as a safer defense against communism than the possible chaos after Balaguer's demise.

Furthermore, even in this case, the role played by the United States was in keeping with the relationship of suprasovereignty. The United States had again taken decisive steps to influence the course of Dominican history. Without Carter's actions, it is likely that Guzmán would not have been inaugurated as president. But whatever its political preferences in that specific matter, the United States had again demonstrated its omnipotence in shaping Dominican outcomes.

Since the watershed election of 1978, the relationship between the United States and the Dominican Republic has shifted from concerns over political development to issues related to trade, investment, drugs, and emigration. The administrations of Jorge and Balaguer maintained relatively good ties with Washington, especially as a result of President Reagan's Caribbean Basin Initiative in 1981, which not only pumped millions of dollars of aid into the country but also created the mechanism for enchanced trade and investment benefits. There were periods of tension during the Jorge administration, particularly over sugar quotas and short-term support for the debt, but these issues never led to a serious break in relations.

During Balaguer's fifth term from 1986–1990, relations with the United States entered a more mature phase, as both countries worked closely to resolve points of difference such as the rising tide of drugs entering the United States from the Dominican Republic and the explosion of illegal immigrants going to the United States. Since his election in 1986, Balaguer has become an unabashed champion of the Caribbean Basin Initiative and has lobbied hard for its extension and expansion. He also has been successful in increasing the sugar quota to the Dominican Republic despite opposition from domestic interests in the United States.[4] Balaguer's mature approach brought dividends in that the Dominican Republic is viewed in Washington and in corporate boardrooms as a solid democracy with a proinvestment economy.

The main sticking point in the relationship has been the serious decline in U.S. assistance to the Dominican Republic. At a time when the country is desperate for development aid and new loan guarantees, the Reagan and Bush administrations have cut aid to the Dominican Republic from $104 million in 1987 to $24 million in 1990. Since his victory in 1990, Balaguer has continued to develop good relations with the United States, although his interest in developing ties with the European community and the countries of the Pacific Basin has also increased. Never one to give the appearance of complete dependency on the United States, Balaguer is clearly seeking to diversify his country's contacts and commitments. For its part, Washington is keeping a close eye on Balaguer despite the amicable relations and the positive business climate. U.S. policymakers are concerned about Balaguer's declining popularity, his failure to resolve long-standing economic problems, and the chance that instability will accompany the transition to a new leadership in 1994 or perhaps earlier.

With the focus of attention in the Caribbean Basin shifting from concerns over Communist expansionism to free trade and regional development blocs, Dominican relations with the United States have shifted from preeminent security concerns to economic cooperation and fiscal reform. Today, the United States is confident that democratic governance has taken hold in the Dominican Republic and that, despite recession and indebtedness, the key issues of the relationship will not be political. But because politics is the lifeblood of the Dominican Republic, the United States cannot ignore the dangers inherent in national strikes, urban unrest, and opposition maneuvering. The relationship between the two nations has clearly changed since the days when the United States unilaterally intervened, engineered elections, pumped aid dollars into the economy, and controlled the terms of dependency. If maturity means that the relationship has progressed to a place where both countries are primarily concerned over how to benefit from closer ties, then, indeed, the Dominican Republic and the United States have entered a new era.

THE DOMINICAN REPUBLIC'S RELATIONS WITH ITS CLOSEST NEIGHBORS

Haiti and Puerto Rico

Although the United States remains the center of most Dominican international attention, there are longer and potentially as important relationships that the Dominican Republic maintains with its most proximate neighbors, Haiti to the west and Puerto Rico to the east.

Dominican-Haitian relations have seldom been cordial. The Dominican Republic has been invaded, occupied and pillaged by the Haitians on numerous occasions since the beginning of the nineteenth century. Haiti, in turn, accuses the Dominican Republic of being a racist nation, slaughtering unwanted Haitians (20,000–30,000 during the Trujillo era), and continuing to import and use Haitians as almost slave laborers. These attitudes have been hardened by stereotypes and have produced hostility, antagonism, and warlike competition.

Although much of the animosity stems from this history of conflict, occupations, and racial prejudice, the more recent problems between the two nations have their roots in a different set of conditions: Dominican development in the face of Haitian stagnation. In the last several decades, the Dominican Republic has made great strides, while Haiti has remained the most underdeveloped nation in Latin America. The autocratic Duvalier family, which has been in power in Haiti since the 1950s, has been unable or unwilling to raise the country's living standards and has used exceedingly repressive tactics to stay in power.

The regime of Jean Claude "Bebe Doc" Duvalier, who succeeded his father, did little to solve that nation's immense problems. Overpopulated, denuded of trees and topsoil, its agriculture largely ruined, Haiti slipped further into the status of hemispheric "basket case" under the younger Duvalier. Its depressed conditions put immense pressures on the Dominican Republic next door. Though the border between the two countries was closed under the Duvaliers, thousands of Haitians streamed into the Dominican Republic to cut cane or to seek employment in the cities. Though legally obliged to return to Haiti, few do so because job opportunities and salaries are so much better on the Dominican side. As illegal immigrants, they have been assimilated into the Dominican population.

The migration of Haitians to the Dominican Republic has, since the 1980s, drawn attention to the working and living conditions of the cane-cutters. Regular studies by the United Nations and human rights organizations have been critical of the treatment of the Haitians. Charges of cane-cutters being held in near-slavery conditions have tarnished the reputation of successive Dominican governments anxious to present a positive human rights image. One study described the conditions of "extreme squalor and depravity" in the camps set up for the Haitians and further claimed that the traffic in cane-cutters is condoned by both the Haitian and Dominican governments. These governments have also been accused of working out an agreement on the fee paid for each Haitian worker rounded up and sent to the Dominican Republic.[5]

Since these allegations were made in the mid-1980s, the Dominican government has claimed to be working to remedy the plight of the cane-cutters and to end the contracting of Haitian workers. Unfortunately, because of the need for a steady flow of cane-cutters, semislavery conditions apparently persist, as do growing tensions between the Haitians and their Dominican bosses over living conditions and pay.

Despite the tensions created by illegal immigration and the charges of collusion in what is almost a slave trade, the two governments have sought to develop better relations. For the first time since 1958, the two countries' leaders met in 1979 to discuss their common problems and common interests. Presidents Duvalier and Guzmán signed an agreement of cooperation and discussed the use of Dominican territory as a base for anti-Duvalier guerrilla attacks. Subsequently, they met again to open a new irrigation project benefiting both countries.

Although Guzmán sought to lessen the tensions with Haiti and develop a sense of normalcy in the relations between the two countries, the upheaval in Haiti that started with the removal of Bebe Doc in 1985 and continued on with the jockeying for power by various military leaders brought an end to what many felt were promising diplomatic and economic overtures. The instability in Haiti made the Dominican government under Joaquín Balaguer wary of Haitian rebel forces opposed to the military using the Dominican Republic as a staging area for guerrilla warfare. Balaguer put his border police on high alert and prepared the country for the prospect of Hispaniola once again being torn asunder by political instability. Fortunately for the Dominican Republic, the turmoil in Haiti did not spill over the border, except in terms of more refugees and an occasional civilian politician or military leaders seeking asylum.

After nearly five years of internal conflict brought about by the unwillingness of the powerful military elite, in concert with the hated paramilitary Tonton Macoutes, to accept popular rule, in 1991 Haiti held its first free election since the days of Papa Doc Duvalier and elected the firebrand priest, Jean Bertrand Aristide. Aristide, a populist with leftist leanings, had a brief tenure as president. Eight months after he assumed office, the conservative military, fearing that the new president was building his own elite military units and encouraging reprisals against repressive military officers, removed Aristide from power and installed a supreme court judge, despite outcries from the Haitian émigré community and vigorous protest from the Organization of American States.

Because of Aristide's past involvement as a strident critic of the Duvaliers, his championing of Socialist causes, and his adversarial relationship with the military, the Balaguer government was cautious about developing close ties with its new democratic neighbor. Moreover, Balaguer has developed a reputation as a Dominican nationalist eager to denigrate Haiti and Haitian culture. Balaguer wrote a widely read book that compared the two countries and clearly placed the Dominicans in a superior position. Yet, despite the animosity that exists between the two countries over racial discrimination, historical events, employment conditions, and social differences, the fact that the island of Hispaniola now has two democratic leaders may provide the impetus for talks that will lead to a more normal and productive relationship.

Future relations between the two countries are tied closely to the future of the Duvalier regime. If internal instability besets Haiti, the Dominican Republic is almost certain to be drawn into the conflict. Such involvement is sure to rekindle the old animosities between two neighbors who have, on a number of occasions, been close to war. At the same time, Haiti's continued nondevelopment, the differences in living standards between the two countries, and illegal immigration into the Dominican Republic also help preserve the age-old prejudices.

Although Dominicans still feel little identification with Haiti, they do have much in common with the neighboring Puerto Ricans. The Dominican Republic has had a long and generally amicable relationship with Puerto Rico. The two islands are separated by a short hop by plane or boat. The Dominicans and Puerto Ricans speak the same language, share the same culture, and vacation or shop on each other's island.

But trade is also a major factor in their relations. Puerto Rico consistently ranks high in import and export trade with the Dominican

Republic. In fact, trade figures show that Puerto Rico ranks fourth as a buyer of Dominican exports, behind only the United States, Spain, and the Netherlands. It also is a major supplier of Dominican imports, and, in recent years, it has worked closely with the Balaguer government to develop joint venture projects and utilize so-called 936 funds, which are monies available to Puerto Rico because its unique tax situation that can be used for investment purposes.

The cordial relations between the Dominicans and the Puerto Ricans should not imply that there are no areas of disagreement or concern. Over the years, fishing limits have provided one bone of contention. The rich Cabo Engaño and Siete Hermanos fishing beds off the coast of the Dominican Republic are worked by both Puerto Rican and Dominican fishermen. The competition has been sufficiently fierce that the U.S. government entered the controversy to work out an acceptable compromise. Dominican leaders tend to play down the disagreement, but the issues of fishing rights and catch ceilings, especially because the prime fishing areas are within the two-hundred-mile limits of both islands, require constant monitoring by the government.

An issue with even more explosive potential is the disparity in living standards between the two islands and, hence, the large number of Dominicans who have migrated to Puerto Rico. San Juan, Puerto Rico, is now thought to be the fourth largest "Dominican" city, behind only Santo Domingo, Santiago, and New York. An estimated 100,000 Dominicans (probably considerably more because many have entered illegally, coming across the Mona Passage by boat at night) have settled in the Commonwealth of Puerto Rico, from which a considerable proportion emigrate again, this time to New York. This last step in the migration process is probably the easiest; to go from Puerto Rico to New York requires only money, credit, or a paid passage—not visas or immigration papers.

Former President Bosch, who himself spent four years of political exile in Puerto Rico, bemoans the deterioration of life in his country that makes such a massive exodus of Dominicans to Puerto Rico or the United States an economic necessity. Although Bosch's comments are connected with his hope that these economic exiles might constitute a force for triggering revolutionary change back in the Dominican Republic, it is important to remember that the Dominicans in Puerto Rico also pose problems for the commonwealth. Despite the much higher per capita income figures in Puerto Rico ($2,250 per year, as compared with the Dominican Republic's $950), the commonwealth also is faced with high unemployment, overextended welfare costs, and acute shortages of housing and human services. The Dominicans living in Puerto Rico thus compete for scarce jobs and services with a population that can ill afford new arrivals. Frequently, the Dominicans take jobs away from Puerto

Ricans because they are willing to work for less. This competition and the potential for ugly conflict concern both Dominicans and Puerto Ricans.

The issue of Puerto Rico's status is also of major interest to the Dominicans. Most government officials, including the president, have not taken a formal stand on the three options open to Puerto Rico—commonwealth, statehood, or independence—preferring to state publicly that it is up to the Puerto Ricans to decide for themselves. Most conservative and centrist Dominicans, however, favor either statehood or a continuation of the commonwealth status, which would have the practical effect of maintaining or increasing the U.S. presence and commitment in the Caribbean. In contrast, the left wing of the PRD and leftists in general support independence for Puerto Rico and are critical of the continuing colonial arrangement that the United States maintains with Puerto Rico. This element clearly favors a diminution of the U.S. presence in the Caribbean—though neither group appears to have thought through the full economic and pragmatic implications of its position.

THE DOMINICAN REPUBLIC IN RELATION TO THE CARIBBEAN AND THE WORLD

Dominican foreign policy is primarily regional and has historically involved relations mainly with the United States and the Spanish-speaking nations in and around the Caribbean. However, in recent years, there has been a surge of new nations in the Caribbean, primarily former British colonies but some former French and Dutch territories as well. This has plunged the Dominican Republic into the larger maelstrom of Caribbean politics. Concurrently, its role in the hemisphere and world at large has also expanded.

Since the 1960s, the Dominican Republic has greatly expanded its international and diplomatic relations. It now has ties with over fifty nations, in Latin America (all the countries except Cuba), Western Europe (all the major countries and most of the smaller ones), the Middle East (Israel and Lebanon), and Asia (Japan, Taiwan, South Korea). There are currently no formal diplomatic relations with any of the former Eastern bloc countries, countries, though there are pressures in this direction and some limited commercial ties are being established.

The Dominican Republic has moved recently to increase its trade with such Latin American nations as Brazil, Mexico, and Venezuela. Of particular interest was the petroleum importation agreement signed with Venezuela, under which the Dominican Republic was given guarantees of uninterrupted supply and favorable loan arrangements to purchase oil. In its expanded ties with Mexico and Brazil, the Dominican Republic is also seeking to diversify its trade and reduce its dependence on Middle Eastern oil. But the Dominicans are proceeding cautiously in expanding trade with Latin America: They have refused to join the Latin American Free Trade Association (LAFTA), preferring to work out trade arrangements on a bilateral basis rather than through the larger multilateral agency.

The Dominican Republic has also expanded its diplomatic and trade relations with a number of the small island nations that previously were crown colonies of Britain. The Dominicans recognize the rising importance of these small states in the area of trade and from the standpoint of political and strategic concerns. To reinforce this new interest in the Caribbean, the Dominican Republic since 1984 has held observer status in the Caribbean Economic Community (CARICOM) and has significantly expanded its trade with neighboring nations such as Barbados, Trinidad-Tobago, and Jamaica. Although partial status in CARICOM has not blossomed into any permanent participation (in large part because of cultural differences and fear of domination by the larger, more diverse Dominican economy), the movement toward regional trade alliances on a par with European unification in 1992 and the emerging North American trading bloc has once again spurred interest in developing a stronger, more expanded Caribbean trading community.[6]

Even with these new Caribbean and Latin American ties, the Dominican Republic has also intensified its efforts to expand its trade with Japan and Western Europe. The prosperity of these nations has given the Dominican Republic the opportunity to diversify its trade and to reduce somewhat its dependence on the United States. Expanded trade has been primarily with Canada, Japan, Germany, the Netherlands, Switzerland, Italy, and Spain; these nations have also considerably expanded their investments, primarily in industry, construction, and mineral exploration, in the Dominican Republic.

The Dominican Republic has supplemented its bilateral relations with substantial involvement in international organizations. The Dominican Republic is a member of the UN, the OAS, the UN Economic Commission for Latin America, the International Labor Organization (ILO), the International Court of Justice, and the IADB. It is also a participant in such financial and business agencies as the International Monetary Fund, the World Bank, the International Finance Corporation, the International Bauxite Association, and the Latin American and Caribbean sugar exporters' groups. The last two are international cartels of commodity-producing nations that hope to do for bauxite and sugar what OPEC has done for oil.

In seeking to understand the Dominican Republic's place in the international sphere, it is instructive to examine the important role it has played in one of these international agencies. The OAS, founded in 1948 as a regional arm of the UN, is charged with helping maintain peace in the hemisphere and promoting economic and social development. The Dominican Republic is a charter member. What is most interesting about the OAS in the present study is the extraordinary amount of attention it has devoted to the Dominican Republic.

No other country except Cuba has been the focus of so much OAS (and thus hemispheric) attention as the Dominican Republic. In 1960, because of dictator Trujillo's efforts to assassinate the president of Venezuela, the OAS for the first time imposed economic and diplomatic sanctions on a member nation. In 1962, after lifting the sanctions, the OAS provided assistance in rewriting Dominican electoral laws and in overseeing the election. In 1963, the OAS interposed itself between the Dominican Republic and Haiti when the two nations seemed on the brink of war. In 1965, the OAS, in what some have called its "darkest hour," submitted to intense U.S. pressure in agreeing to create the Inter-American Peace Force, which helped control the Dominican revolution and provided a facade of hemispheric multilateralism to what was really a unilateral U.S. intervention. In 1978, the OAS was again involved in Dominican affairs when it protested the seizure of the ballot boxes by Balaguer supporters. Finally, during the Central American crisis, the Dominican Republic, working with the OAS, participated in the ill-fated attempt to bring the Nicaraguan dictator Anastasio Somoza and the Sandinista rebels together as a means of halting the destruction and bloodshed, later in 1987, it served as a site for peace talks between the Sandinistas and the contras.

The OAS gained much of its experience in international peacekeeping, the application of sanctions, and similar matters through its various Dominican experiences. Many Dominicans would have preferred that such experience be acquired at the expense of another country.

RECENT TRENDS IN DOMINICAN FOREIGN POLICY

The increased participation of the Dominican Republic in the Latin American community of nations, its widening ties to Europe and Asia, and its respected role as a peacemaker in the region has lifted the nation to a position of prominence it has not enjoyed since the early 1960s. In a 1979 survey, conducted by a New York research firm, of 208 government, academic, and business leaders in the United States, the Dominican Republic was rated the second most important country in the Caribbean, behind only Cuba. President Guzmán was, that year, listed as the fourth most important political figure in the region, behind Castro, Jamaica's Michael Manley (defeated in the recent elections), and President José López Portillo of Mexico. But Guzmán was only a scant 1 percent behind

López Portillo and significantly ahead of Venezuela's Luís Herrera Campins.

Such recognition is enormously important to the Dominicans, who take great pride in their nation having finally achieved its place in the sun. National, recognition, in turn, reflects the stability, economic development, and democratic government achieved since the critical election in 1978, of which the Dominicans are also immensely proud. The next great milestone for Dominican pride is certain to be the 1992 celebrations of Columbus's arrival in the New World. The Balaguer government is counting on considerable attention, as international leaders and dignitaries are scheduled to visit the Dominican Republic during these celebrations. The government has sent precious development dollars on refurbishing historical monuments and expanding the nation's tourist capacity, but its main interest is in showing the world that democratic stability and an invigorated economy are firmly in place in the Dominican Republic.

The growing prominence and involvement of the Dominican Republic in Latin American affairs and its increased ties to the advanced industrial world come at an interesting time. The rise of the regional and global economies, the demise of communism, the maturation of the relationship with the United States, and the push for new and innovative economic arrangements have transformed the Dominican Republic into a nation that wants to be at the leading edge of the changes that are engulfing the world. Political and business leaders are convinced that this country can play a key role in developing the Caribbean into an economic center equivalent to the Pacific Basin. With the extension of the Caribbean Basin Initiative by the U.S. Congress in 1990, the export opportunities provided by the Lome IV Accords in the European community, the heightened interest in Dominican export processing zones by an ever-widening range of international investors, and the prospect of hemisphere free trade zone reaching from Alaska to Tierra del Fuego have combined to create a mood of confidence and a real sense of progress and movement in the country.

As this book's title implies, the Dominican Republic lies in the center of this Caribbean crucible. For years, the region was primarily viewed as one of immense strategic importance, but the changing world order has pushed the Caribbean and the Dominican Republic into the next frontier of economic development and business opportunity. The lessening of ideological tensions, the de-emphasis on defining the area in geopolitical terms, and the sense that democratic governance has finally brought a level of stability and respectability to the Caribbean have joined to redefine the region as something more than a "trouble spot"—its traditional title. Fidel Castro may still be close by, drug trafficking and the violence that goes with it may remain, and the political unrest brought on by inequality and injustice may be an integral part of everyday life, but the Dominican

Republic, like its neighbors, is putting on a new face in an attempt to ensure that the changed world that is fast emerging does not pass it by.

The Dominican Republic may not become a regional power or power broker, but its ability to maintain democracy amidst adversity, its attractive investment policies, and its sustained efforts at change and modernization have given it a reputation that is certain to enhance its influence in the region. More importantly, the willingness to change and open the nation to the global economy will provide the foundation for the eventual transformation of this sugar republic into a significant center of economic enterprise.

The international position of the Dominican Republic provides both problems and opportunities. The initiatives of the Guzmán government laid the groundwork for amicable relations with neighboring countries and strengthened the nation's own position in the region and the world. But the emergence of the Caribbean as an area of renewed importance and potential danger puts the Dominican Republic in a precarious spot. It may mean a chance for the country to further its stature and influence, or it may force it into an ideological and superpower struggle that could threaten its independence and recent accomplishments and force it to reevaluate its crucial relationship with the United States.

10

Conclusion

The Dominican Republic has had a troubled past. Its considerable natural resources were milked dry by the Spaniards, and its native Indian population was decimated. It then suffered through some three centuries of colonial neglect, during which its institutions and political forms decayed and its social and economic structures reverted to more primitive subsistence forms. Manipulated and bartered by the great powers, both historically and presently, it has seldom had control of its own destiny.

Its history as an independent nation is as tumultuous and ruinous as its colonial history. First, it was occupied and devastated by the Haitians. Then, a succession of domestic tyrants—Santana, Báez, Heureaux, Trujillo—dominated its politics and its national life, with often disastrous consequences for the country. In between, there were occupations by Spain and the United States, immense internal turmoil, an occasionaly ineffective democratic leader, and a lack of economic development.

After Trujillo's assassination, the Dominicans again sought to achieve democratic growth. But the government was overthrown after only seven months, graft and oppression reappeared, and, in 1965, the country exploded in revolution and civil war—only to see its hopes for a democratic restoration crushed once more by U.S. intervention.

The Dominican Republic remains a poor country. The gaps between rich and poor are vast. It has immense social and economic problems. Its resources are terribly limited. It is vulnerable to forces over which it has no control.

But the Dominicans are a proud and persevering people. In the twenty-seven years since the civil war, they have made immense strides. On a slim resource base, still heavily dependent on the United States, they have nevertheless made enormous progress toward economic development, social reform, and political democracy. This progress, in the face of the severe problems they must overcome or live with, has been both remarkable and heroic. The hatreds and fragmentation occasioned by the

Columbus lighthouse (*courtesy of the Dominican Republic Tourism Promotion Council*)

1965 revolution, civil war, and U.S. intervention have been ameliorated over time.

The accomplishments of the past three decades are still tenuous, however, and the situation could change very rapidly. The threats to democracy from the armed forces and reactionary elements are strong and very real. The country remains torn by social tensions and divisions. The economy remains precarious and would suffer devastating blows if oil prices increased dramatically or if sugar prices declined. Despite all its efforts at development and diversification, the economy is still subject to the whims of world market prices.

Although the Dominican Republic has changed a great deal in the last twenty-seven years, the question of whether these changes have been sufficient to alter its basic behavioral patterns must remain an open one. For instance, the two historical currents that have always vied for dominance in Dominican politics, the authoritarian one and the liberal-democratic one, are both still very much alive (as personified by the governments of Trujillo and Bosch or Balaguer and Guzmán); one could not say with any certainty that the latter has definitively superseded the former. The trend, however, has been toward democracy.

Alongside these two main currents, a third and potentially equally important one has appeared: the force of revolutionary socialism. At present, that force remains weaker than the other two, but that may only be because the Dominican Republic is less developed than Chile or Argentina, let us say; and it is possible that, in the future, sentiment in favor of a more radical restructuring will grow. Hence, though the Dominican Republic may have passed one hurdle with the restoration in 1978 of democratic government, it is conceivable that the growth of a more revolutionary challenge to the status quo will produce both increased conflict and polarization *and* call forth a renewed authoritarian response, as in many other Latin American countries.

Much depends on the economy. If it continues to expand, the Dominican Republic may be able to continue on a democratic course and head off a revolutionary explosion. But should the economy turn stagnant, stop expanding, or even shrink, then the political order will be gravely threatened.

Much also depends on the changing nature of Dominican society. Since Trujillo, the Dominican Republic has become considerably more affluent and considerably more middle class. Some observers argue that these changes militate against future political upheavals because too many Dominicans have too big a stake in things to risk losing all in a major confrontation. We are not sure this new affluence and "middle classness" in the society will produce the stability envisioned. Such changes may raise expectations for even greater change, rather than dampening them. And though the middle class may be a force for stability, it is also deeply divided; in defense of its interests, a large sector of the middle class could come to favor a repressive regime.

But the Dominican Republic is changing and doing so at an accelerated rate. The new affluence, new social programs, the emerging middle class, and economic development are all altering the face of the landscape—physically, psychologically, and politically. The Dominicans are beginning to achieve that place in the sun to which they have always aspired, and what we find particularly interesting and worthwhile are their efforts to diversify their trade and economic relations and thus modify the conditions of dependence under which they have always existed.

If the key to breaking out of the interlocking vicious circles of underdevelopment is to attack all of them simultaneously, to modernize the economy while also diversifying, to reduce dependency while also recognizing hard international realities, to solve social problems while also building up capital for investment, and to institutionalize political democracy but to do so in accord with home-grown values and practices, then the Dominican Republic in the last twenty-seven years seems to have come a considerable distance. Also impressive are the country's efforts to expand democracy and build a more democratic political system, fashioning that system in accord with Dominican desires and traditions.

Notes

CHAPTER 2

1. Dominican geography and topography are discussed in detail in Thomas Weil et al., *Area Handbook for the Dominican Republic* (Washington, DC: Government Printing Office, 1973), pp. 9–17.

2. The Dominican Republic has recently undertaken a major program to extract gold and silver from the area in and around Pueblo Viejo. See *Times of the Americas,* October 30, 1991, p. B3.

3. See Shelby Coffey, "Letter from the Dominican Republic," *Washington Post,* March 30, 1984, p. E1.

4. Ian Bell, *The Dominican Republic* (Boulder, CO: Westview Press, 1981), p. 17.

5. See Pedro Andrés Pérez Cabral, *La comunidad mulata: El caso socio-politico de la República Dominicana* (Caracas: Grafica Americana, 1967). See also Franklin J. Franco, *Los Negros, los mulatos y la nacion dominicana* (Santo Domingo: Ed. Nacional, 1969).

6. For a discussion of the impact of Trujillo on Dominican life, see Howard J. Wiarda, *Dictatorship and Development: The Methods of Control in Trujillo's Dominican Republic* (Gainesville: University of Florida Press, 1970).

7. Michael J. Kryzanek and Howard J. Wiarda, *The Politics of External Influence in the Dominican Republic* (New York: Praeger, 1988), pp. 63–65.

CHAPTER 3

1. See Frank Moya Pons, *Historia colonial de Santo Domingo* (Santo Domingo: Universidad Catolica Madre y Maestra, 1974).

2. See Rayford Logan, *Haiti and the Dominican Republic* (New York: Oxford University Press, 1968).

3. The depiction of the era of the "dual caudillos" is best accomplished in Hugo Tolentino Dipp, *La traición de Pedro Santana* (Santo Domingo: Impressos Brenty, 1968).

4. For a discussion of the Heureaux era, see Howard J. Wiarda, *The Dominican Republic: Nation in Transition* (New York: Praeger, 1968), p. 30.

5. Fred J. Rippy, "The Initiation of the Customs Receivership in the Dominican Republic," *Hispanic American Historical Review* 17 (November 1937), pp. 419–457.

6. The most comprehensive and balanced study of the U.S. occupation is Bruce J. Calder, *The Impact of Intervention: The Dominican Republic During the U.S. Occupation of 1916–1924* (Austin: University of Texas Press, 1984).

7. The authoritative biography of Trujillo is Robert Crassweller, *Trujillo: The Life and Times of a Caribbean Dictator* (New York: Macmillan, 1966).

8. G. Pope Atkins and Larman Wilson, *The United States and the Trujillo Regime* (New Brunswick, NJ: Rutgers University Press, 1972).

9. Bernard Diederich, *The Death of the Goat* (Boston: Little, Brown, 1978).

CHAPTER 4

1. For a discussion of the Council of State era, see John Bartlow Martin, *Overtaken by Events: The Dominican Crisis from the Death of Trujillo to the Civil War* (Garden City, NY: Doubleday, 1966), pp. 155–177.

2. Juan Bosch, *Crisis de la democracia de America en la República Dominicana* (Mexico, DF: Centros de Estudios y Documentacion Sociales, 1964).

3. The best account of the civil war and the U.S. intervention can be found in Piero Glejesis, *The Dominican Crisis: The 1965 Constitutional Revolt and American Intervention* (Baltimore: Johns Hopkins University Press, 1978).

4. For a discussion of the regionalization of the peacekeeping forces in the Dominican Republic, see Jerome Slater, *Intervention and Negotiation: The United States and the Dominican Revolution* (New York: Harper and Row, 1970), pp. 142–153.

5. Abraham Lowenthal in *The Dominican Intervention* (Cambridge, MA: Harvard University Press, 1972) discusses the reasons for the Dominican intervention by the Johnson administration and the debate over the wisdom and success of the action. See especially pp. 132–145.

6. James Nelson Goodsell, "Balaguer's Dominican Republic," *Current History* 53, no. 315 (November 1967), pp. 298–302.

7. Howard J. Wiarda and Michael J. Kryzanek, "Dominican Dictatorship Revisited: The Caudillo Tradition and the Regimes of Trujillo and Balaguer," *Revista/Review Interamericana* 7, no. 3 (Fall 1977), pp. 417–435.

8. See Michael J. Kryzanek, "Political Party Decline and the Failure of Liberal Democracy: The PRD in Dominican Politics," *Journal of Latin American Studies* 9 (1977), pp. 115–143.

9. Michael J. Kryzanek, "The 1978 Election in the Dominican Republic: Opposition Politics, Intervention and the Carter Administration," *Caribbean Studies* 19, nos. 1 and 2 (April–July 1979), pp. 51–73.

10. See Jan Knippers Black, *The Dominican Republic: Politics and Development in an Unsovereign State* (Boston: Allen & Unwin, 1986), pp. 62–63.

11. Jonathan Hartley, "A Democratic Shootout in the D.R.—An Analysis of the 1986 Election," *Caribbean Review* 15 (Winter 1987), pp. 14–16.

12. Rosario Espinal, "The 1990 Elections in the Dominican Republic," *Electoral Studies* 10, no. 2 (1991), pp. 139–144.

CHAPTER 5

1. The most complete analysis of the Dominican social structure is contained in Howard J. Wiarda, *Dictatorship, Development and Disintegration: Politics and Social Change in the Dominican Republic* (Ann Arbor, MI: Xerox University Microfilm Monograph Series, 1975).

2. A helpful discussion of rural life and politics can be found in Kenneth Sharpe, *Peasant Politics: Struggle in a Dominican Village* (Baltimore: Johns Hopkins University Press, 1977).

3. The most contemporary analysis of the Dominican military is G. Pope Atkins, *Arms and Politics in the Dominican Republic* (Boulder, CO: Westview Press, 1981).

4. See Rosario Espinal, "Labor, Politics and Industrialization in the Dominican Republic," in *Economic and Industrial Democracy*, vol. 8 (London: Sage, 1987), pp. 183–212.

5. A list of U.S. business and private organizations in the Dominican Republic can be found in the annual publication of Caribbean/Central American Action, entitled *Caribbean and Central American Databook* (Washington, DC: Caribbean/Central American ACTION, 1991).

6. See José Luis Alemán, S. J., "Transformaciones de la democracia en la sociedad contemporanea," in La democracia dominicana: Experiencia y desafios, *UNIBE* 1, no. 1 (Enero–Abril 1989), pp. 1–13.

CHAPTER 6

1. Aaron Segal, "King Sugar Is Ending Reign," *Times of the Americas,* September 12, 1984, p. 10.

2. *The Dominican Republic Foreign Economic Trends Report,* U.S. Embassy, Santo Domingo, August 15, 1990, pp. 10–11.

3. See the publications of the Dominican Export Promotion Center, Dominican Mission in the United States, 1 Madison Ave., New York.

4. *The Dominican Republic Labor Trends, 1989–1990,* U.S. Embassy, Santo Domingo, 1990, pp. 2–3.

5. For an overview of Dominican export promotion and foreign investment attraction, see Kal Wagenheim, "New Foreign Investment Spurs Dominican Economy," *Wall Street Journal,* special advertising section, June 22, 1978, p. 1.

6. The progress made in Dominican tourism is discussed in *Business Week,* special advertising section, April 4, 1988, pp. 6–8.

7. See our discussion of the impact of international assistance on the Dominican economy: Michael J. Kryzanek and Howard J. Wiarda, *The Politics of External Influence in the Dominican Republic* (New York: Praeger, 1988), pp. 161–165.

8. See *Report by the U.S. State Department on the Caribbean Basin Initiative, May 1989*, prepared by the Office of Regional Economic Policy, Bureau of Inter-American Affairs, Department of State.

CHAPTER 7

1. See Rosario Espinal, *Autoritarismo y democracia en politica dominicana* (San José: CAPEL, 1987).

2. For a more recent discussion of Balaguer and his governing style, see Mark Kurlansky, "In the Land of the Blind Caudillo," *New York Times Magazine*, August 6, 1989, pp. 24–30, 43.

3. Bringing real reform to the Dominican government was not an easy task, as shown by Richard Kearney's "Spoils in the Caribbean: The Struggle for Merit-Based Civil Service in the Dominican Republic," *Public Administration Review* (March/April 1986), pp. 144–151.

4. See Jan Knippers Black's discussion of Balaguer's ties to the Christian Democratic Party, *The Dominican Republic: Politics and Development in an Unsovereign State* (Boston: Allen & Unwin, 1986), pp. 84–87.

5. The support for Juan Bosch and the PLD is discussed in Kurlansky, "In the Land of the Blind Caudillo," pp. 26–28.

6. The early relationship between the PRD and Balaguer is discussed in Michael J. Kryzanek, "Diversion, Subversion and Repression: The Strategies of Anti-Regime Politics in Balaguer's Dominican Republic," *Caribbean Studies* 19, nos. 1 and 2 (1979), pp. 83–103. For a more recent analysis of the relations between the PRD and Balaguer, see Rosario Espinal, "The Defeat of the Dominican Revolutionary Party in the 1986 Elections: Causes and Implications," *Bulletin of Latin American Research* 9, no. 1 (1990), pp. 103–115.

7. *Amnesty International Reports, 1988* (London: Amnesty International Reports Publications, 1988), pp. 108–109.

CHAPTER 8

1. See Kal Wagenheim, "Dominican Republic Agribusiness Diversifies from Traditional Crops," *Wall Street Journal*, special advertising section, June 22, 1978, p. 1.

2. Paul R. LaTorture, "NeoSlavery in the Cane Fields—Haitians in the Dominican Republic," *Caribbean Review* (December 1985), pp. 18–20.

3. See Miguel Ceara Hatton, "Crisis economica y democracia: Hacia una economia de espumas," *Ciencia y Sociedad* 12, no. 2 (Abril–Junio 1987), pp. 246–261.

4. *Times of the Americas*, November 26, 1986, p. 8.

5. See Michael J. Kryzanek, "The Dominican Republic," in Jack Hopkins, ed., *Latin America and Caribbean Contemporary Record, 1984–1985* (New York: Holmes and Meier, 1985), pp. 695–704.

6. A helpful study of the migration issue is Eugenia Georges, *The Making of a Transnational Community: Migration, Development and Cultural Change in the Dominican Republic* (New York: Columbia University Press, 1990).

7. See the analysis of the Dominican energy situation by Juan Lara in *Latin American Economic Outlook—The Dominican Republic*, WEFA Group, June 14, 1990, pp. 12.3–12.5.

8. See *Country Marketing for the Dominican Republic Plan, 1989*, U.S. Department of Commerce, Washington, DC, pp. 10–11.

CHAPTER 9

1. A classic study of U.S. intervention in the Dominican Republic is Sumner Welles, *Naboth's Vineyard: The Dominican Republic 1844–1924* (New York: Payson and Clarke, 1928).

2. See, for example, Carlos Maria Gutíerrez, *The Dominican Republic: Rebellion and Repression* (New York: Monthly Review Press, 1972).

3. The election of Balaguer in 1966 is often viewed as a "demonstration election"—democratic form with little popular substance. See Edward S. Herman and Frank Broadhead, *Demonstration Elections: U.S. Staged Elections in the Dominican Republic, Vietnam and El Salvador* (Boston: South End Press, 1984).

4. Tom Wicker, "Disastrous Sugar Diplomacy in the Caribbean," *New York Times*, March 14, 1987, p. A27.

5. Pamela Constable, "A Yearly Harvest of Shame in Hispaniola," *Boston Globe*, May 18, 1986, pp. A1, A4.

6. See Henry Goethals, "Free Trade in the Western Hemisphere: A Threat or Challenge?" *Times of the Americas*, May 29, 1991, p. 13.

Suggested Readings

Atkins, G. Pope. *Arms and Politics in the Dominican Republic* (Boulder, CO: Westview Press, 1981). A contemporary study.

Atkins, G. Pope, and Wilson, Larman C. *The United States and the Trujillo Regime* (New Brunswick, NJ: Rutgers University Press, 1972). A thorough, scholarly study.

Bell, Ian. *The Dominican Republic* (Boulder, CO: Westview Press, 1981). Good historical and socioeconomic analysis.

Black, Jan Knippers. *The Dominican Republic: Politics and Development in an Unsovereign State* (Boston: Allen & Unwin, 1986). A critique of the Dominican "system."

Bosch, Juan. *The Unfinished Experiment: Democracy in the Dominican Republic* (New York: Praeger, 1964). An account by the former president.

Calder, Bruce. *The Impact of Intervention: The Dominican Republic During the U.S. Occupation of 1916–1924* (Austin: University of Texas Press, 1984). Excellent historical study.

Crassweller, Robert D. *Trujillo: The Life and Times of a Caribbean Dictator* (New York: Macmillan, 1966). An excellent biography.

Georges, Eugenia. *The Making of a Transnational Community: Migration, Development, and Cultural Change in the Dominican Republic* (New York: Columbia University Press, 1990). Important examination of critical aspect of Dominican experience.

Gleijeses, Piero. *The Dominican Crisis: The 1965 Constitutionalist Revolt and the American Intervention* (Baltimore: Johns Hopkins University Press, 1978). Scholarly yet sympathetic to the rebels.

Haggerty, Richard A., ed. *Dominican Republic and Haiti: Country Studies* (Washington, DC: Government Printing Office, Federal Research Division of the Library of Congress, 1991). A fine overview.

Hendricks, Glenn. *The Dominican Diaspora: From the Dominican Republic to New York City* (New York: Teachers College Press, Columbia University, 1974). Good background study of migration issue.

Hillman, Richard S., and D'Agostino, Thomas J. *Distant Neighbors in the Caribbean: The Dominican Republic and Jamaica in Comparative Perspective* (New York: Praeger, 1992). An excellent comparative study.

Kryzanek, Michael J. "Political Party Decline and the Failure of Liberal Democracy: The PRD in Dominican Politics," *Journal of Latin American Studies* 9 (1977), pp. 115–143.

————. "Diversion, Subversion and Repression: The Strategies of Anti-Regime Politics in Balaguer's Dominican Republic," *Caribbean Studies* 17, nos. 1 and 2 (1977), pp. 83–103. This and the following are among the few serious studies of the Balaguer regime.

————. "The 1978 Election in the Dominican Republic: Opposition Politics, Intervention and the Carter Administration," *Caribbean Studies* 19, nos. 1 and 2 (1979), pp. 51–73.

Kryzanek, Michael, and Wiarda, Howard. *The Politics of External Influence in the Dominican Republic* (New York: Praeger, 1988).

Lowenthal, Abraham F. *The Dominican Intervention* (Cambridge, MA: Harvard University Press, 1971). Serious, balanced.

Martin, John Bartlow. *Overtaken by Events: The Dominican Crisis—From the Fall of Trujillo to the Civil War* (Garden City, NY: Doubleday, 1966). Long, fascinating account by a well-meaning U.S. ambassador.

Rodman, Selden. *Quisqueya: A History of the Dominican Republic* (Seattle: University of Washington Press, 1964). Readable but dated.

Sharpe, Kenneth Evan. *Peasant Politics: Struggle in a Dominican Village* (Baltimore: Johns Hopkins University Press, 1977). Good, interesting.

Slater, Jerome. *Intervention and Negotiation: The United States and the Dominican Revolution* (New York: Harper and Row, 1970). The best account of these events.

Walker, Malcolm T. *Politics and the Power Structure: A Rural Community in the Dominican Republic* (New York: Teachers College Press, 1972). An interesting case study.

Wiarda, Howard J. *The Dominican Republic: Nation in Transition* (New York: Praeger, 1968). An earlier general overview.

————. *Dictatorship and Development: The Methods of Control in Trujillo's Dominican Republic* (Gainesville: University of Florida Press, 1970). An analysis of the dictatorship.

————. *Dictatorship, Development, and Disintegration: Politics and Social Change in the Dominican Republic* (Ann Arbor: Xerox University Microfilms Monograph Series, 1975). Much background and detail.

Wiarda, Howard J., and Kryzanek, Michael J. "Dominican Dictatorship Revisited: The Caudillo Tradition and the Regimes of Trujillo and Balaguer," *Revista/ Review Interamericana* 7 (Fall 1977), pp. 417–435. A comparative study.

About the Book
and Authors

Much has occurred in the Dominican Republic since the first edition of this critically acclaimed profile was published ten years ago: Democratic government has become more firmly established, if no less contentious, and the fragile economy, though still the definitive element in Dominican life, has benefited from changes in global trade patterns and corporate investment. Yet the Dominican Republic remains a nation mired in poverty and social tension. As the country heads toward the quincentennial of Columbus's landing in the New World, there is both anticipation and apprehension as the citizenry looks back proudly to their heritage and forward to a future clouded by uncertainties.

This edition examines the changing character of governance and the political changes that have returned Joaquín Balaguer to the presidency for an unprecedented sixth term. The economic transitions that have made the Dominican Republic an attractive site for foreign business and tourism are also addressed, along with the economic causes of urban and rural unrest and the emigration of Dominicans to Puerto Rico and the United States. Critical public policy issues such as energy, taxation, population control, and education are explored, together with the social and political conflicts created by debt, austerity, and fiscal reform. Finally, the authors analyze the Dominican Republic's relations with its neighbors and major trading partners, giving special emphasis to the impact of new global and regional ties. Throughout, they focus on the struggle to maintain democracy in the face of the inevitable dislocations caused by economic reform and modernization.

Howard J. Wiarda is professor of political science at the University of Massachusetts–Amherst (on leave), professor of national security studies at the National Defense University in Washington, D.C., and visiting scholar at the Center for Strategic and International Studies. **Michael J. Kryzanek** is professor of political science at Bridgewater State College in Massachusetts and in 1990 was visiting scholar at Boston University's Center for International Relations. One of his most recent books is *Leaders, Leadership, and U.S. Policy in Latin America* (Westview, 1992).

Index

and Puerto Rico, 141
and Reformist Party, 105
relations with United States, 76,
135–137
response to protest, 67
and Social Christian Reformist Party,
106
social welfare policies of, 119–120
style of leadership, 48, 110
support for democracy, 111
tax policies of, 129
and Trujillo, 105
Balagueristas, 50
Barbados, 143
Baseball, 18
Batista, Fulgencio, 135
Bennett, Tapley, 43
Betancourt, Romulo, 37
Bill of Rights, 109
Bonao, 9
Bonnelly, Rafael, 41
Bosch, Juan, 1, 2, 40, 46, 63, 96, 100,
101, 103, 141, 148
and anti-government
demonstrations, 67
and Dominican Liberation Party, 106
and election of 1982, 51
and election of 1986, 52
government of, 41–42
and liberal democratic coalition, 105
and middle class, 65
opposition role, 54
and United States, 135
Boyer, Jean Pierre, 27
Brazil, 1, 83, 142
Britain, 26, 29
British, 27, 31
Bush, George, 76, 93, 94

Caamaño Deno, Francisco, 43, 45
Cabarete, 15
Cabo Egano, 141
Cacéres, Ramon, 31, 32, 103
Campesinos, 61
Canada, 143
Caribbean, 1, 5, 133

Caribbean Basin Initiative, 76, 93, 94,
137, 145
Caribbean Economic Community
(CARICOM), 143
Carter, Jimmy, 50, 54, 134
Casa del Campo, 13
Castro, Fidel, 39, 40, 144, 145
Castro Communists, 23
Castroism, 135
Catholic Church, 54
and divorce, 72
and family planning, 72
See also Catholicism
Catholicism, 20
Caudillo, 21
Central Bank, 87, 90, 119
Central Election Board, 53
Central Romana, 74
Chamber of Deputies, 101
Chile, 1, 149
Cibão Valley, 6, 30, 31, 47, 59, 62
Civil war of 1965, 2, 42–46
Class, 17, 66–69
Coca-colaization, 17–18
Colonial economy, 26
Colossus of the North, 134
Columbus, Christopher, 5, 23, 25, 145
Columbus, Diego, 12
Columbus lighthouse, 86, 148(photo)
Conquistadores, 26
"Constitutionalists," 42, 44
Constitution of 1966, 109
Cordilleras, 6
Corruption, 104
Costa Rica, 44, 110
Council of State, 40, 46
Cuba, 1, 5, 26, 42, 70, 136, 142, 144
Culture, 20–21
Currency devaluation, 84

Debt, 84
Democratic development, 149
Democratic leadership, 103–104
Democratic Quisqueyan Party (PQD),
108
Demography, 9